The Emergence of I

How the Universe Woke Up

BY JOHN PAYNE

Book Cover by Andrew Magee

Published by Payneful Publishing, LLC, Chicago.

Contents

PART I:
THE FALL

CHAPTER 1:

I Am That

Each of us has in our own life at least one moment of insight, one Mount Sinai—an uncanny, other-worldly, time-stopping experience that somehow succeeds in breaking through the grimy, boisterous present, the insight that, if we let it, will carry us through our life.

~ Thomas Cahill[1]

I was That.

A pile of dried cherry wood lay next to the dying fire. Bars of night silver beamed through an auditorium of paper birches and aspens, illuminating the open space around the pit. Heavy silence blanketed the forest. Howls from a night creature in the distance perforated the quiet. Three companions stared into the depths of the fire, transfixed as the unspeakable unfolded before them.

Icy needles pierced my flesh, breaking my trance. I watched fractal structures of snowflakes collapse against my skin, acquiescing to the heat of mammalian blood. Then the boundary between my skin and the air dissolved, and an eerie sense of familiarity rushed through my body.

My gaze returned to the fire pit. The glowing pieces of wood had somehow relocated. The sense of familiarity grew to an eerie been-here-before. Déjà vu. Something I've always known. Someplace I've always been. A time I knew would come. Foresight and remembering at once.

I glanced between snowfall and fire as the primitive hierophany continued. Amputated arms of charred wood dissolved and reformed into different positions before my eyes. One moment they lay flat, the next they tilted against each other, and then seemed strewn across the fire pit— arranging themselves in desperately random positions. Some invisible trickster had taken charge of their assortment; my companions and I had not touched them. The fire pit glowed lazily, exhaling drowsy wisps of smoke from its center. And then suddenly it would awaken, dancing tongues of flame into the air without aid of wind, and then fall dormant again.

Everything in the world felt like it was somehow going on in here inside of me, not happening somewhere out there. The snowing and the burning felt like breathing or digesting, somehow automatically governed by my body, whose boundaries somehow no longer ended at the edge of my skin but included the entire world.

Raw fear prickled up the back of my neck. Am I responsible? Am I making it snow? Am I doing all of this? Impossible. Yet at the core of my being I knew it to be true. Some inner watcher was lucidly and soberly observing and accepting the impossible.

Time dissolved. The past and the future collapsed into the present and the eternity of Now became forcefully obvious. Every moment occurred at once. Everything in the universe was occurring right now. Simultaneity. All whens, all wheres. I was occurring as That, with That. No past. No future. No birth. No death. Right now. Forever.

I was undone, dissolved into the Whole. My psyche flipped inside out. My mind cracked open, and the contents of my entire life spilled out into the ether, spread bare for the witness of my two companions. Every memory of my life blended together in the Now, psychically out loud: every beating, every tear, every hello, every goodbye, every first, every last, every high, every low, every regret, every thrill, every severed friendship, every disappointment, every victory, every failure, every love, every broken heart, every shame, every orgasm, every grudge; my weakness, my strength, my hope, my hopelessness. The faces of every person I loved flashed before my mind in an instant, one after the other, as different facets of one Being. As me. Is this all just me? I thought. A fresh tingle of fear surged up the back of my neck. I swallowed hard and said nothing. The "I" had broken under the full weight of reality.

I felt dead. I was dead. And somehow I knew the feeling. I was sure of it. The familiarity with the death state was so unforgettably peculiar. How could I know that feeling? I have never been dead before, I thought. But then the absurdity of that unexamined assumption struck me. Feeling dead felt good. It felt like ecstasy, like final release.

With knowing dread, I looked up at my companions. Their eyes were twisted with the same fear and awe. They had lost their minds too. They too were witnessing the manipulation of physical reality by an invisible manipulator. They too were swimming in an ocean of raw experience and immediate memory. They too felt the ecstasy and terror of death. And behind the fear in their eyes, I saw something impossible yet so plain and obvious: I. I saw myself. And looking back into my eyes, they saw the I, too. They saw themselves. No words were spoken because none were needed. Psychic union. At last. Home. I felt like I was back, back to where I belonged, back to where I came from, back to a place I clumsily let fall between the couch cushions. Oh, here it is! Silly me. How could I have forgotten about this place? It felt like remembering.

So this is what insanity feels like. My sanity was payment for clairvoyance. I felt for the first moment in my adult life absolutely necessary to reality. My mind was calling reality into existence. Reality was, I realized, a projection of my mind. Well, not John's mind, but a mind, the Mind, perhaps. The mind I was occupying in that moment seemed to be a mind beyond age, a mind at large, maybe older than the planet, perhaps as old as time itself. And this Mind, which included me somehow, too, was doing it all. Reality felt like dreaming aloud. And much like in a dream, my mind admirably performed the part of willing co-conspirator, flagrantly disregarding reason, natural law, and logic. The snow, the fire, the logs—all of it performed by the sly trickster behind the curtain.

A thousand insights streamed through me, too fast and too many to grab hold of for safekeeping, but one epiphany was so obvious and so clear and so undeniable as to be unforgettable. The great cover-up of the Western psyche had been revealed to us, as it has been to the many who have experienced the numinous mysterium, the unfaceable truth and the blackest taboo of our culture. The hilarious and terrifying secret had been whispered into my ear. I laughed and I cried.

I was That.

What you just read was my attempt to describe one of the most profound experiences of my life. I have in some ways never recovered from it. I struggle to put the episode into words. I borrow the easiest simplifications like Totality, Enlightenment, Eternity, mystical experience, Nirvana, and God, but, as everyone who has had this experience knows well, words fall short of conveying its meaning and depth in a satisfying way to themselves or others. Many times I played the enthusiastic fool in front of a sober jury of friends or strangers. And understandably so. Why should they care? What was in it for them?

Getting across *my* experience is not important. What I want to get across is another way of seeing the *human* experience. What *are* we doing here? What *is* here? And how did we get here? These questions are only understood to the extent that man can understand himself. Instead of seeing ourselves as a species of chemically accidental sacks of flesh on some irrelevant rock on the outer edge of an endless void, perhaps we might see ourselves as the most central and important thing the universe ever conceived. After all, it is eerie that your experience is happening—of all places throughout the cosmos—through this ape body on this apparently accidental planet.

Calling ourselves unimportant and peripheral or explaining away our existence as the byproduct of the careless and blind forces of nature, is a popular trend today. But it is due time we acknowledge that this kind of put-down is at best a tired holdover from the wave of scientific reductionism of the nineteenth century. At worst it is an unexamined attitude of self-hatred masquerading as fact-facing, scientific realism. It is also entirely irrelevant to a very plain fact: you are here. What could be more direct, urgent, immediate, or important than that? What could be more meaningful?

Let's start with a question: why is it now? I type these words at 9:33 a.m. on December 5th, 2022. But why are you reading these words right now? You're here against all odds. Of all the time that has gone by since the beginning of the universe, of the two-and-a-half-million years of human existence, of the entire two-hundred-fifty-thousand years that *Sapiens* has roamed the earth, of the ten-thousand years since humans gathered themselves into small, farming communities, of the five-thousand years of recorded history, you, somehow, someway, of all the billions of people to ever exist, are reading these words in the twenty-first century. In terms of sheer chance of existing, you may as well win the lottery every minute of every day. Why wasn't this lifetime spent experiencing reality as *Australopithecus* or *Homo Erectus* or *Homo Neanderthalis*? Why aren't you camped half-naked around a fire in 40,000 BC? The fact that you are here and now living out what is apparently your single lifetime is either an incredible coincidence or we need a new way of looking at reality.

Picture a spherical grid that's constantly expanding, like an explosion that goes on indefinitely. This is a common conception of the universe today (and one in some sense pictured by some of the ancient Greek philosophers). We'll call this sphere-grid Awareness. At various locations inside of Awareness, knots of little sub-awarenesses weave together. The knots are never separate from the sphere-grid. No matter how intricate their weave is, the strings of each knot tie into the sphere-grid's overarching frame. It is ultimately one structure. Think of this image a model of the universe: a huge, infinite sphere containing varying degrees of awareness throughout.

In the beginning, the first knots to form inside of the sphere-grid weave simply, forming balls of gas and rock like stars and planets. As time goes on, tighter and more intricate knots of awareness form. And then on a certain rock inside a certain star system within a certain galaxy, basic chemistry turns into biology. Simple life appears. First, it's prokaryotes for about two-billion years. Then it's eukaryotes. Compared to the primitive gas and rock knots of before, these weaves of Awareness are sophisticated.

The next stage of Awareness to emerge is complex life. Awareness now centralizes itself into a variety of knots with very sophisticated weaves. Animals appear. And then shortly after that a bizarre form of complex intelligent life arises, a very special type of ape called various names, but we'll call it *Homo*. Like most knots of awareness of the intelligent-life variety, the *Homo* knot is of a tight and complex weave but, at least at first, not substantively different from anything else in its biological class. But just two-million years after its appearance, a very short period of time for Awareness, the *Homo* knot cinches tightly into an intense, shining point of awareness—the most intense point of view in all of material existence, so far as we can tell. And through the eyes of this ape, the universe wakes up to itself and knows. *Aha! I am here. I am.* And right now at this moment it is reading the words on this page.

You are experiencing this moment in the twenty-first century because two inches behind your forehead is one of the most intensely centralized, self-reflecting points of view the universe has ever concocted. Across all simultaneous moments throughout all of time, the universe is currently experiencing itself at your coordinates because that is where it is most aware. This is not to say that other lifeforms on other planets do not exist or to discount the degrees of self-awareness in other animals. Self-reflectiveness is a spectrum, and humans appear to be sitting at the top. You are not experiencing yourself as *Australopithecus* or *Homo Erectus* because neither were as intensely self-aware and self-reflective as you.

Your special point of view exists as a function of both body and culture. The bodily hardware of life that makes this point of view possible developed through a long process of biological evolution, over three-and-a-half-billion years. The software—the way you consciously think, feel, and act, your worldview—was coded by over a hundred-thousand years of cultural evolution. The story of human history—both prehistory and recorded history—is not just a linear series of events, people, and places. It is not just a random walk out of Eden into farming, urbanization, and industrialization. It is more aptly the story of how the universe reflected on itself—a story of increasing self-awareness, a rise of self-consciousness out of the dark ocean of the collective Unconscious. The story of everything, the story of *you*, is the creation of a point of view, of subjective experience. The story of humanity's descent into civilization is the story of the articulation of the ego.

CHAPTER 2:

A New Historical Perspective

At the still point of the turning world
Neither flesh nor fleshless
Neither from nor towards
At the still point, there the dance is
But neither arrest nor movement.
And do not call it fixity
Where past and future are gathered...
Neither movement from nor towards
Neither ascent nor decline.
Except for the point, the still point,
There would be no dance
And there is only the dance.
I can only say, there we have been
But I cannot say where
For that would be to place it in time.

~ *T.S. Elliot*

To carry us down the historical river from the Paleolithic to the present, we will use three rafts to stay afloat. The first is the relationship between the Self and ego, the second: the relationship between the left and right brains, and the third: the relationship between language and consciousness. Together they form the themes of this book and will help us see history as an evolution of awareness instead of as a stream of causality.

We typically prefer to look at the past from the latter perspective. One event causes another which causes another which leads to another and so on. There is nothing *wrong* with seeing history this way. But just so, there is nothing *wrong* with seeing history as an evolution of consciousness. These two perspectives are not mutually exclusive. They are just two different ways of looking at the same happening. We can see the past as a gradual development of awareness, an inevitable constriction of consciousness from the Big Bang to you. Instead of assuming that the present is a result of the past, we should see that the past is a result of the present. In other words, the past is created by the present. When has it been any other time but Now?

Ego means *I* in Latin. It is what I think of as *me*. It is a symbol for the general sensation of being inside my skin, the feeling of being separate from everything else. My ego-consciousness rises out of an awareness of my personal past and future. In this sense, it is an identity. It is an identity concocted by the Self of itself.

The Self is the center of experience. It incarnates as you, me, my mother, your neighbor's dog, and any extraterrestrial inhabiting distant galaxies.[i] Each Self feels itself as the center of the universe. In that sense, the ego is awareness of awareness, a hyper-focused central point, a center of centers. The process of the ego emerging out of containment within the Self is a process called individuation. Microcosmically, individuation is the process of maturing out of childhood into adulthood whereby one becomes an individual. Macrocosmically, this process is how the universe woke up.

Another important dualism we will rely on to build our perspective in this book is left brain versus right brain. Using a McCluanesque line of thinking, Leonard Shlain proposed that

---

[i] Some threads of Hindu philosophy distinguish between ego (ahamkara), the Self (Atman) and the universal psyche (Brahman).

preliterate societies were right-brained, venerating feminine values, the Goddess, holism, and images, whereas literate cultures, specifically those that invented or embraced the alphabet, revered the masculine in lieu of the feminine, adopted linear thinking, monotheism, and male-dominant modes of rule.

The left/right brain dichotomy roughly corresponds to that of the ego and Self in that the ego represents the cognitive point of view of the left brain, whereas the Self equates to the cognitive lens of the right brain. And most importantly for our discussion, the exclusively left-brain specialties of language and literacy lie behind the rise of ego-consciousness.

Once we see human history as a process of evolving consciousness, we can then recognize the hidden pattern in history's tapestry and its connection to ourselves. If, for a moment, you suspend the assumption that time is linear—that there is a beginning, a middle, and an end, or a past, present, and future—the only alternative you are left with is that time is a holistic, eternal Now. From this standpoint, instead of a horizontal, causal chain of separate events, things, and individuals from the beginning of time until its end, what we get is a vertical continuum of change, one continuous flow of indistinct form occurring in the Now. Individuals or separate things and distinct events do not exist from this perspective because nothing is linearized: it is happening together at once. The Big Bang did not happen billions of years ago. It is happening.

The structure of the universe is analogous to a novel. We typically read novels in a linear fashion, following the events of the story from beginning to end. But in fact, despite how we may choose to read it, the novel is a unit, a complete whole, and the story exists all at the same time. We are free to open the book at any page we wish and move forward or backward from there. All the scenes and chapters exist all together, not one at a time. The story only seems to exist sequentially. But in the mind of the author, it exists as a complete whole. The characters in the story represent the ego, each unaware of the whole story, living out their individual spans of time linearly. The author of the story, then, is the Self. It creates each character but contains the entire story in its mind at once as a living whole.

If this is hard to digest, consider this question: when did you come into being? At what point did you separate from your mother and become a separate thing? If you burrow into this question, you'll find that a satisfying border between your two beings cannot be established. Was it when you emerged from the womb? Was it during the first trimester? Was it at conception? Was it when your parents had sex? At what point did you *begin*? All of these designations are arbitrary. They are discrete points of abstraction assigned by an intellect onto an unbroken process of a continuous happening. And if taken to its furthest depths, the simple answer is that you never began because you never ended.

This is why the illusion of the ego is so incredibly impressive. I certainly feel separate from everything else. But this is not really the case. It is a matter of language. It is built into our grammar—subject, object, nouns, verbs with their past, present, and future tenses. Language is the engine of ego-consciousness because when language and especially literacy are learned, they psychically build the ego and separate it from its environment.

Although language does not leave behind a trail of hard evidence, humans have probably been speaking since *Homo Erectus* and *Homo Habilus*. But the unique head shape and unusually short oral cavity of *Homo Sapiens* suggest that our powers of speech and language could be exclusive to our species.[1] No appreciable level of consciousness can occur without language.

Language is a tool that we use not only to reflect on the world, but to produce the world itself. As the anthropologist

Misia Landau notes, "...language is not merely a device for communicating ideas about the world, but rather a tool for bringing the world into existence in the first place. Reality is not simply 'experienced' or 'reflected' in language, but instead is actually produced by language."[2] Prior to the linguistic revolution, we navigated the world in an unconscious state of dim self-reflection. But then the human mind began separating itself from the matrix of nature. Using language as an implement of thought, our mind divided the world into pieces.

"As language," Eric Havelock tells us, "became separated visually from the person who uttered it, so also the person, the source of the language, came into sharper focus, and the concept of selfhood was born."[3] Self-reflection is not unique to humans. There is a growing pile of evidence showing that other animals like chimpanzees, dolphins, whales, and elephants can and do self-reflect in ways we have not yet fully appreciated. But orcas do not build New York City. By 50,000 BC, human beings were self-reflecting in a way no other animal had before or has since. We routinely buried our dead, decorated our bodies with clothing and ornaments, and exhibited some of the earliest signs of religion. Language allowed us to rise out of the torrential ocean of information that reality is and reassemble it into conscious relationship with ourselves. It woke us up to the notion of time. And only a being with a sophisticated grasp of time could adequately confront the temporal challenges of agriculture, which is the basis of civilization.

Language articulates and objectifies reality. This is not to say that no external world exists and that this is all a matter of speech. There is an external world. But the contents of that external world are configured and set into relationship with us by the assumptions and conventions of language that we call grammar.

Look around you right now. You are surrounded by language. Table, cup, sun, tree, lake, sink, floor, ceiling, chair, red. Reality is draped in words, but behind the draping is...what, exactly? What if these objects did not have a name? What would they be? This is difficult to think about at first. What is the essential nature of the cup? You could say the cup is really just porcelain, but this just replaces "cup" with another word. You might go further and say that the porcelain is made up of trillions of atoms, but "atoms" are yet another set of letters, and so we are no closer to actual reality than before.

How we think of ourselves in relationship to the cup is based on the rules of language. *I touched the cup.* Implicit in that sentence is a sequence of time in which a subject (*I*) takes action (*touched*) upon an object (*cup*). The grammar in this case not only objectifies reality by divorcing subject (*I*) from object (*cup*), but the tense of the verb also places the event in the past. We could tweak the sentence to just as easily put the event in the present or the future. Our sense of linear time—our past, present and future—is reinforced by language.

Language helps us make distinctions in reality that are, on a deepest level, not distinct at all. The Hindus insist that the words of Sanskrit are the roots of the actual things in the world. Everything, their tradition holds, comes into existence by *Vak*, which is speech. For the Chinese, *Tao* originally meant speech, the creative principle that calls the world into existence, much like the Christian *Word* or Greek *Logos*. Before the mind names or numerates it, the world hangs suspended in a state of chaos. It snaps into definite position—a thing—when the instrument of thought is applied. Our grammar eventifies and thingifies space-time, cutting it into pieces. We encapsulate segments of time and, just like we do with things, name them as a means of crystallizing them. Making a sandwich, World War II, the financial crisis of 2008, and the formation of the solar system are events cut from an eternal Now.

Language gives rise to ego and culture; culture and civilization intensify language and ego. The ego screens reality through a filter of culturally proscribed attitudes, feelings, cues, possibilities, and expectations (such as a perspective or a worldview). The ego, in this way, is a linguistic abstraction through which consciousness interacts with the universe or, more precisely, with itself. The birth of civilization may be seen as a graduation party for the evolution of ego-consciousness, since civilization is a kind of separation from nature. As Chuang Tzu said,

> "The knowledge of the ancients was perfect. How perfect? At first they did not know that there were things. This is the most perfect knowledge; nothing can be added. Next, they knew that there were things, but did not yet make distinctions between them. Next, they made distinctions between them, but they did not yet pass judgements upon them. When judgements were passed, Tao was destroyed."[4]

From a human perspective, the story of ego-consciousness is a torrential river of awareness flowing down from the distant Paleolithic through the Neolithic periods that forked into the two great tributaries we know today as Western and Eastern civilization.

Both the West and the East inherited a sense of self out of the shared cultural background of the Neolithic. The differences between the West and East are profound, if only because they are complementary. The West went down the cerebral path. It champions logic and linear thinking. It is characterized by abstract thinking, analysis, individualism, and reason. Things are best understood by looking at their particulates, and so naturally the Western mind classifies, categorizes, speciates, and divides. Nature is seen as created, made, and ordered by an authoritarian force, or subject to immutable scientific laws. Either way, nature is governed. Time flows linearly from past to present to future. The individual is honored, celebrated, and worshipped in the West. In many ways, the ego has become a special, psychological elaboration of Western civilization.

The East, on the other hand, is corporeal. Intuition, instinct, and holism characterize many of its traditional attitudes. *We* is emphasized over *I*. Consensus is sought, uniqueness flattened. Harmony and sameness are preferred to difference and variance. Reality is best understood through relationship, not separation. Nature is seen as a self-ordering, decentralized organism; there is no cosmic boss or universal law calling the shots from behind the scenes. Such is the *Tao*. Time is holistic, rather than linear. Whereas the West places perhaps a disproportionate amount of value on the individual, group identity is perhaps overvalued in the East. In America the squeaky wheel gets the grease; in China the loudest duck gets shot first.

Today's *I*, the ego that I am ultimately concerned with, is invariably a Western construct. Globalization is considered by many to be the Westernization of the world, for better or for worse. And after suffering humiliation and military defeats at the hands of the West during the last two centuries, the East downloaded Western military, economic, and cultural systems to incredible effect. This is not to say that the Eastern mind is fully Westernized or that its essence has not penetrated the West. While globalization does seem unidirectional, that may only be because the infiltration of Eastern values into the West is mainly invisible to the West. Yoga, meditation, Zen buddhism, holistic medicine, harmony with nature rather than rule over it—these are Eastern values that have been exported to the West at the precise historical moment we need them most.

But where does the Western worldview come from? How was it built? To answer this question we have to look at the cultures fundamental to the West: the Greeks and the Hebrews. Western civilization's roots extend down into both, whose languages form the core of the Western mind. All the languages of the West, and an increasing number of languages globally, use the Roman alphabet, which was taken from the Greeks, who developed it from the Phoenician-Canaanite-Hebrew model.

The Greeks and the Hebrews gave the West its psychological filter, the essential makeup of its point of view. The way we perceive time, space, matter, and each other come from the Greeks and Hebrews. While the Greeks gave us rationality, logic, atoms, musical and visual aesthetics, and categories of thought, the Hebrews gifted us psychology, morality, history, and the individual. At the beginning of the Common Era, these worldviews merged and had a profound, formative effect on the psyche of Western civilization and its egos.

By appreciating the formation of ego, the West can become aware of the ego's illusory essence and *re-collect* itself into a unified whole. This hope is not to be confused with yet another attempt at a New Age treatise on the evils of ego. And it is not to say the West should abandon its most precious gift of individualism. On the contrary, the West should continue to embrace individuality and revivify its liberal values. But if it wants to do that, it must realize that the beauty and highest expression of individuality thrives only when it is understood to spring from something greater than itself. Genuine individuality is an expression of an underlying unity. The individual turns rigid and grotesque when that is forgotten. It fossilizes into its past or gets lost in anticipation of its future. The result is a hyperventilating panic that prevents us from getting a grip on our world problems.

CHAPTER 3:

Wandering in the Garden

I couldn't be that important,
as far as I could see.

But you make me feel
The universe is alive.
All bees in one hive.

And that it's living
just for me.

You plunge from the top of a skyscraper toward concrete; prickles run up your neck as you open a creaky door at the end of a darkened hallway; nails split the lid of the coffin you lay paralyzed inside of. Needles cascade up your spine, and a ball of ice forms in the pit of your stomach.

You awaken in a panic, covered in sweat. Relief washes over you. It was just a dream.

As real as dreams feel, the words *truth* and *dream* are seldom associated. Taken below their pandemonium, however, we acknowledge a certain *je ne sais quoi* about dreams. Suddenly recalling a weird dream from the night before gives pause. For at the center of dreams we acknowledge a certain meaning, a nugget of raw truth dripping with the liquid of our deeper psyche. They give off an alien, yet somehow eerily familiar scent from the depths of our soul. And yet by the time we've made it to the bathroom in the morning, the rational mind has dismissed the memory, brushing off the twilight circus show as the babbling of an unregulated mind.

But though dreams are irrational, this does not make them unreal. Whether individual or collective, dreams are facts. It is time to begin paying attention to both our personal and collective dreams, for they have much to tell us.

One such collective dream of the West is the Garden of Eden. Believer or non-believer, secular or religious, educated or not, everyone knows the image of the naked couple and the serpent in paradise. Passed down from the Sumerians to the Babylonians, then to the Hebrews who conferred it on the West, this story captures the collective mind of every age. Each era interprets the myth differently.

For the modern age, the myth of Eden represents, among other things, the moment the universe woke up to itself through mankind. Eden is a spatial-temporal metaphor for a fundamental state of animal cognition, an unconscious mindset embedded in the woven fabric of nature. It is the image of us innocently wandering through a verdant rainforest, blissfully unaware of self, intuiting existence and interacting peacefully with other forms of life. Across the entire Bible, only in Genesis do an animal and a human communicate (the serpent and Eve).[i] The fact that this kind of discourse never repeats tells us that whatever occurred in Eden constituted an irreversible shift that transformed the proto-Paleolithic ape, Adam, into something beyond itself.

Adam's transformation is triggered by the famous act of disobedience. God commands: "From the Tree of the Knowledge of Good and Evil, you are not to eat, for on the day you eat from it, you must die."

Adam and the woman eat from the tree anyway, at the serpent's suggestion. The serpent tells the woman: "Die? You

---

[i] The second biblical example occurs in the book of Numbers when a donkey speaks to Balaam, but it is God who speaks through the donkey. In Genesis, the serpent speaks its own thoughts.

will not die! Rather, God knows that on the day you eat from it, your eyes will be opened, and you will become like gods, knowing good and evil." In fact, after eating from the Tree of Knowledge, "the eyes of the two of them were opened, and they knew then that they were nude."

This story signifies the moment the universe began to reflect on itself through man, a motif elaborated and iterated throughout the Old Testament. Adam and Eve do not die in the immediate physical sense of the word, but rather become self-aware to the extent that they, like us, are able to anticipate the inevitability of death. In other words, they ascend out of the experience of original, unconscious bliss, of eternal time, into ego-consciousness and linear time. Death became a new reality *through* the ego. In order to manifest, the ego dualizes existence into opposites: life and death, light and dark, pain and pleasure, good and evil, I and thou. But in so doing, the ego must then confront the reality and terror of its inevitable dissolution.

Adam represents our state of innocence as the collective, proto-Paleolithic hominin unable to reflect genealogically on itself as a series of individuals. He is the primal, unconscious continuum of experience of the common man, the man or "human" common to us all, residing fully in the Now. In this sense, pre-expulsion Adam is the Total Human before its breakage into generations and lineage. Time and death are only real to the individual. Awareness of one's birth, or beginning, and the anticipation of one's death, or end, are experiences unique to a being that can reflect and think itself separate from its predecessor and successor.

In Genesis, the apparent contradiction between the supreme deity's warning of death and the serpent's counsel toward a state of higher awareness is reconciled in the transformation of Adam and Eve from unconscious hominins into ego-conscious human beings. The difference between Adam and Eve and every other human thereafter is that Adam and Eve were created by God, not born. They were immortal until they became aware. Death is the universe's price for becoming man. The serpent and God were both right.

What is the point of holding onto the fairytales of our ancient predecessors? Wouldn't we be better off if we could divest ourselves of these ancient holdovers? At our own peril, we dismiss our archaic myths as naïve attempts by our primitive ancestors to grasp the true workings of reality. With this myopia, we not only lose the opportunity to appreciate the worldview of the myth-makers, but also the chance to peer into the evolution of our own consciousness. Joseph Campbell said that dreams are "the personalized myth" and myth is "the depersonalized dream."[1] If that is so, then myths must be "attempts by society's dreamers to find a language to penetrate to the heart of reality," as Thomas Cahill so beautifully put it. And myths must also be attempts to plumb the mysterious depths of ourselves. Myths carry us over what Trumbull Stickney called "meaning's edge" into the yawning abyss of *That*, the unsayable.[2] From this perspective, we can begin to see mythology not as naive bedtime stories or failed explanations of nature but as a collective treasury of raw truths about being human.

Arguing over literality—whether the grain goddesses actually brought fertility to the fields, whether Yahweh built Adam out of clay, or whether Prometheus' liver was really eaten every day by an eagle—is to miss the point. Myths are not necessarily rational. They are symbolic, not of facts in the world, but of that which is inexpressible. They are images through which humans relate to reality. And the function of myth, ancient or modern, is to jump our minds past the phenomenal world—the experience of waking ego-consciousness—to truth. The purpose of *ontological* myths is to put us in contact with everlasting Truth. Plotinus called this leap "the flight of the alone into the alone."

Since the purpose of myth is so poorly understood by the Western mind today, it is important to juxtapose myth against science, history, theology, and metaphysics. Imagine a series of concentric circles. At the center is the inexpressible Absolute, equivalent to the eternal Now. Immediately surrounding it is the realm of myth and metaphysics. Myths are images that point to the inexpressible: the world as it *is,* prior to our division of it into nouns by rational intellect and language. Occupying the same level as myth is metaphysics. I have placed it on the same tier as myth because it also points at and hovers directly above the Absolute. *Meta,* meaning *beyond* or *behind,* and *physic,* meaning *nature,* together mean that which is beyond or behind nature: the foundation of reality. As a subject of study, metaphysics refers to the ground upon which all knowledge rests. A metaphysical *experience* is therefore mystical because it is an experience of the world directly as it is without the interference of linguistically borne distractions of parts of speech (nouns and verbs) and time (tenses).

Theology, in the outer third circle, combines myth and metaphysics, dogmatizing them by treating them as facts that occur in history. Once Christian theology crossed this line, its clash with science became inevitable. As soon as Christian theology declared God a thing, even the greatest thing beyond things, and announced that its myths were events that *happened* as factual occurrences within history, it not only drained both God and their mythology of life, but opened both to fatal autopsies by modern science—which is, ironically, a product of Christian theology born out of this misstep. In the outermost (fourth) circle, science and history describe the phenomenal world of facts and time; they have nothing whatsoever to say about the world in its *unreflected* state because they are fundamentally *reflective* systems of knowledge.[ii]

Whatever everlasting truth underlies reality, it is and always will be what Alfred Korsybski called the *unspeakable world.* And

[ii] For concise definitions of myth, theology, science, metaphysics, and Western metaphysics, I suggest Alan Watts, *Myth and Ritual in Christianity,* (Boston: Beacon Press, 1968), 62-65.

for the last century, Western man has attempted to reveal this world through a grand, unified, scientific theory. But we're looking in the wrong place with the wrong toolkit. The truth we seek is an inner *experience*, not an idea or some final, intellectual scheme of the universe.

Levy-Bruhl termed this experience *participation mystique.* Owen Barfield called it *original participation.* The Hebrews called it Eden. The Greeks called it the Golden Age. The Zen masters call it *satori.* The Hindus call it *nirvana* or *moksha.* A failed replication of it was the first-generation Matrix simulation program that humanity's "primitive cerebrum kept trying to wake up from" as explained by Agent Smith to the captured Morpheus in the first release of *The Matrix* film franchise. We unconsciously recall it as a collective, nostalgic memory of bliss and human childhood, and today we clamor for its return in the form of state-sponsored utopias.

Adam and Eve do not represent two individuals, but a continuum of experience that was one day split into man and woman and broken into genealogy. If they do represent some distant stretch of man's preconscious past, this is not to say that our primitive ancestors were dim-witted Flintstones. In fact, they were probably better-tuned to the natural environment in many ways than we moderns. Humanity was still experiencing itself as undifferentiated from nature, in wholeness with its environment. There was little or no ego to transcend the experience of Now and reflect on time as a chronological stream of past experiences and future anticipations. Experience was *objective.* The biological death of one's companion did not involve the prenotion of one's own death as well. We have gained much from rational ego-consciousness, but have also given up much.

This is also not to say that primitive man was somehow living in an illogical dream world. On the contrary, just like us, they behaved logically in accord with their assumptions about the world. After spending time with primitive societies in

Papua, New Guinea, Carl Jung understood this.[3] What moderns would regard as the chance occurrences of nature—for instance, lightning striking a village or a leopard killing a person—a primitive person would regard as intentional acts. A sorcerer was behind the lightning strike, or a shaman morphed into a leopard and targeted that particular victim.

We naturally criticize this reasoning as superstitious and naïve. But explaining to a preliterate person that these catastrophes happened due to "natural" blind chance rather than intention really would explain nothing at all. Perhaps nature seems chaotic, blind, and random to us because we feel so separated from it. Getting stung by a hornet after leaving your house in the morning for work would probably not ruin your plans for the day, nor would it gain you the approval of your boss to skip work. To a preliterate, however, reality feels deeply interconnected with oneself, so the hornet sting *means* something. It must be an ill omen, and ignoring it would be a serious mistake. All plans for that day should be canceled. Without a strong ego, the internal and external worlds mix together in an undifferentiated swirl of meaning, synchronicity, and connection.

To Paleolithic man the objects of the world were not felt externally as, say, this book in your hands, but rather were blended together as internal contents of a unified psychic state. In other words, there was not yet a conscious and separate relationship between the human individual and the totality of existence encasing it.

CHAPTER 4:

The Reptile Within

If you are going to outwit the devil, it's terribly important that you don't give him any advance notice! Because even if you serve notice privately on yourself that suddenly you're going to drop it all, already the devil knows—because who do you think the devil is?

~Alan Watts[1]

According to Genesis, the serpent is the cleverest of all beasts. The serpent is a symbol of the primitive core of our brains, the unconscious mind, and the trickster-figure within us. For the irony behind the whole Eden story is that we did it to ourselves; in the end, the serpent was an externalized aspect of our psyche onto which we projected our guilt at being.

We tricked ourselves into becoming ego-conscious. Consider that according to Christian legend Lucifer's sin was spiritual pride, and the penalty for it was expulsion from Heaven. Spiritual pride is a commonly misunderstood sin. But it becomes understandable when thought of in relation to Adam and Eve's disobedience in Eden.

As we discussed, the story of Adam and Eve is about ego-consciousness. Ego-consciousness is identification with personal memory and expectation. Taking up mental residence in the past or the future manifests the illusion of self-consciousness and in turn the accompanying illusion of free will. Free will is the fantasy that the abstraction called *I* can choose to act in or out of accord with the fundamental process underlying existence (i.e., God). Here, man commits the sin of spiritual pride. He then finds himself in a double bind because he believes the same *I* that has willfully fallen out of accord with the universe can put itself back into compliance by its own remedial acts of contrition or humility. In this belief too he commits the same sin. This vicious loop in which the sinful *I* tries to correct itself, only exacerbates self-consciousness because these corrective attempts intensify the illusion! Spiritual pride therefore produces self-consciousness because it entraps *I* in a chamber of its own endless reverberation of will and self-correction.

And so the story goes that Adam the naked Anthropos turned away from the Eternal Now and abstracted its sense of self out of memory and anticipation of its future. Adam ignores the present moment and thus ignores the presence of God, clinging to the island of personal will out of fear of its destruction. The preference of personal will to that of the cosmic will is both man and Lucifer's original sin, a kind of pride that precipitated their fall or expulsion from an original state (Eden or Heaven). In this way, Lucifer and gross self-centeredness have always been deeply connected.

It is also for this reason that Lucifer is the "light bringer" because he brings out the light by opposing it as darkness. In the same manner that light lacks definition without darkness, the cosmos lacks definition without ego-awareness. As the *morning star,* Lucifer illuminates the world out of the darkness of its own unconsciousness. He is you, your ego, aware of the world by realizing its pieces and events. The devil must be given his due.

Some of the oldest images of serpents date back to 16,000 BC. It is an original and powerful motif that reaches far back into the Paleolithic Period. It is carved onto sacred stones and tumuli, it appears on the staff of Orthodox Christian clerics, and even American medicine today uses the well-known Caduceus, a rod of two intertwined serpents surmounted by a pair of wings, as a symbol of healthcare, though by mistake.[i]

[i] The correct association is the Rod of Asclepius, which was a staff entwined by a single serpent wielded by Asclepius, the Greek god of healing and medicine.

Biologically, the serpent motif can be seen as symbolic of the evolution of the human brain and the interaction of its parts. There are three primary sections of our brains that evolved in succession over the course of evolution: the reptilian core, the limbic system, and the neocortex.[2] The core is the oldest of the three, having evolved hundreds of millions of years ago. It is responsible for primal functions, like breathing and heart rhythm. We share this primitive brain stratum with reptiles and possibly all other vertebrates. Wrapped around the reptilian core is the limbic system. It includes the amygdala, hypothalamus, and hippocampus and evolved over a hundred-fifty-million years ago. The limbic system is responsible for emotion, memory, body temperature, the fight-or-flight response, hunger, and thirst. Finally, resting atop these two systems is the neocortex. Unique to mammals, the neocortex specializes in abstract thinking, language, planning, and reasoning.

The right-hemisphere of the neocortex was dominant during man's primitive era. This makes sense because the right brain is evolutionarily older than the left. Hemispheric lateralization between the two brain-halves occurred tens of millions of years ago, but the functional differentiation between the right and left is a more recent phenomenon. Over the last few million years of human existence, our brains not only enlarged in size but specialized the left half to manage functions apart from the right, such as language and linearization of time for long-term planning. Evolutionarily recent enlargements in the human prefrontal cortex and the temporal lobes suggest selection pressure for cognitive functions like language and planning. Although the neocortex evolved tens of millions of years ago, its most intense elaboration occurred in primates, dolphins, whales and, most of all, humans. It is the part of your brain that makes you human.

The left side of the brain contains the values the West fundamentally cherishes (almost without examination). It is considered the conscious part of the brain because it is responsible for speech, reasoning, linear thinking, abstract thought, and rationality. Its modes produce the type of thinking needed for military strategy, science, business, and logic. It controls the right hand. We use the word "right" in an evaluative sense for that which is true or good. The pure in spirit sit at the right hand of God. The left hand, controlled by the more unconscious right brain, is traditionally associated with evil. The modes of the right brain are associated with feminine attitudes.

The reptilian brain and limbic system manage the primal as well as the emotional and survival functions of the body. The three inborn fears of infant baboons—falling, darkness, and snakes—are governed by this area of the brain. A baboon mother does not have to teach her infant to fear them. Grabbing the wrong branch fifty feet above the forest floor and falling prey to snakes or nocturnal predators were perpetual risks faced by our primordial, tree-dwelling, primate ancestors. Carl Sagan speculated that these instincts were shaped into existence by millions of years of evolutionary pressure and then are somehow genetically retained into the present. If primal fears ramify through the monkey evolutionary tree of life, what other residues of its past could humanity harbor in its collective mind? Where might we find expressions of these residues?

Consider this cosmic, origin story from Aristophanes' fifth-century BC play *Birds*:

> "At the beginning there was only Chaos, Night, dark Erebus [Darkness], and deep Tartarus [Abyss]. Earth, the air, and Heaven had no existence. First, black-winged Night laid a germless egg in the bosom of the infinite deeps of Erebus, and from this, after the revolution of long ages, sprang the graceful Eros [Love] with his glittering golden wings, swift as the

> whirlwinds of the tempest. He mated in deep Tartarus with dark Chaos, winged like himself, and thus hatched forth our race, which was the first to see the light. That of the Immortals did not exist until Eros had brought together all the ingredients of the world, and from their marriage, Heaven, Ocean, Earth, and the imperishable race of blessed gods sprang into being. Thus our origin is very much older than that of the dwellers in Olympus."[3]

Winged creatures that lay eggs, a new race of beings capable of seeing "the light"...are these extraordinary images connected to the emergence of mammals out of the reptile family and the accretion of its newer brains? "The light," which this new race of beings could see, was preexistent, waiting to be sensed. Maybe it took a more advanced antennae—like a more sophisticated brain—to finally pick up on preexisting stimuli and achieve the novel form of reality that we call ego-consciousness. Evolutionary biologists confirm that both mammals and birds evolved out of reptiles. In our story the primordial gods who precede the humanesque Olympians, like Zeus and Athena, have wings and hatch out of eggs. Perhaps they represent our distant reptilian antecedents in the evolutionary tree of life. Either that or we have to consider, as Sagan did, the somewhat alarming notion that science's conclusions about the biological sequence of life actually depend on these myths, or that they at least emanate from the same source as the myths themselves.

The latter case is the most likely. The eerie thing about myths is that we do not know where they come from. When Jung asked a medicine man where the morning tradition of spitting into his hands and offering them up to the sun originated, the medicine man told him that it had always been done that way.[4] Just like the mother baboon who need not teach her babies to fear heights, darkness, and snakes but couldn't know from where those instincts come, an ancient shaman or priestess would not have known the source of their society's myths and rituals. Freud and Jung said that these come from the unconscious, but this is not an easily understood location. What we do know is that the image or the deed or the ritual always come first, and the action of reflecting on why they exist, what they mean, or how they came to be, comes later. As a rule, life acts first and thinks about it after the fact.

In both Genesis and Aristophanes' *Birds*, reptiles precede or preside over the moment consciousness emerges. In Genesis, it was a serpent, "more subtle than any beast of the field," who initiated contact with humanity and conferred secret knowledge upon them. In *Birds*, the race that hatched out of an egg who could sense "the light" emerged long before the Olympians. And it was the serpent in Genesis who conveyed its secret knowledge of the world to the woman (before she was called Eve), but not to Adam.

The woman's special relationship with the serpent represents the aeon-old connection between the right hemisphere and the reptilian brain. Whatever it must be like to experience existence solely through the window of the reptilian brain core, it is far from a human experience. If one of the functions of the neocortex is to give rise to our sense of self, the feeling of "I," separateness, the epicenter of conscious attention between our eyes, then the reality experienced by the reptilian core and limbic system must veer toward the undifferentiated, the instinctual, the rawness of pure being—enmeshed within environmental interconnection, something like a dream. The brain core is our biological bridge into the primal language of existence, weaving our feeling into the collective experience of life. The neocortex, especially the left brain, separates the organism from the matrix of nature so that it becomes conscious of it.

During a dream, the most active parts of the brain are the right hemisphere and the lower, primitive, brain regions.[5]

The analytical left brain idles in a state of low-level, passive observation, while the intuitive and holistically perceiving right brain surges, producing the dream. The interaction between the right hemisphere and the primitive brain during the dream state may explain the dream's prevalence of emotion, aggression, images, arousal (sexual and otherwise), euphoria, the limited availability of rational analysis, a general absence of abstract signs such as words, and a weak sense of individuality.[6] Are these not the modalities of a wild creature?

A wild animal with a nonexistent repertoire of symbolic language must interact with the world through its intuition. When it finds a stream, an animal does not see *water,* it sees liquid reality. When we dream, we are in a sense regressing to a childhood state. We are reverting to a time when our fragile sense of self was buffeted to and fro by seemingly magical forces and our sense of time was eerily bereft of causality, instead full of connected synchronicity. Is this the cognitive domain of our age-distant reptilian ancestors and near to that of the waking reality of our Paleolithic parents?

Could the interplay between the feminine right brain and its elder reptilian sister, the reptilian core, create something like the gestalt, pictographic experience of our primal past? After all, non-linearity of events and a shaky sense of self-control is neither comfortable nor fathomable territory for the left brain. In a modern society entranced by left-brain values, perhaps our tendency to dismiss dreams as meaningless brain-static, and myths as naïve, cultural holdovers, is projected frustration... frustration of the left brain over inadequately comprehending and verbalizing the irrational, pictographic message jointly generated by its elder sister and her reptilian companion.

CHAPTER 5:

Old Dreams: Hunter versus Goddess

In primitive belief, no animal can be killed against its wish. When a member of a species is struck down, the One is wounded. The hunted animal is seen to give itself to the hunter, as human food, while its spirit returns to group form. Because men did all the large-game hunting and felt themselves to be tracking and slaying brother and sister animals, magic children, like themselves, of Mother Earth—we know they felt guilt, and sought its resolution.

~ *Monica Sjoo and Barbara Moor*[1]

It would not be until earliest 150,000 BC or latest 50,000 BC that *Sapiens'* ego began to appreciably crown from the womb of the unconscious. From this time to roughly 10,000 BC, people began doing things to suggest a more conscious orientation of themselves inside of time. They buried their dead, made jewelry, sewed clothing, used tools, and created art. One important way humans developed a conscious relationship with time was by observing the moon phases.

The moon was a point of collective, human, self-reference. The constant waxing and waning of the moon gave humans a yardstick with which to measure differences and observe repetitive patterns in nature, such as the cycle of seasons, and life and death. Humans may have used the moon to elaborate linear time out of eternity. Lunar notations that correspond to the moon's thirteen cycles have been found engraved on bones, antlers, and ivory figurines dating back to 40,000 BC. These discoveries compelled Alexander Marshack to propose that the foundations of civilization, such as writing, agriculture, mathematics, and calendrical systems, should be understood not as sudden inventions of the historical period, but as culminations of a gradual, cognitive process initiated by Paleolithic man.[2]

The two great myths of the Paleolithic Period are that of the hunter and that of the Goddess. Many cave paintings, like the ones at Lascaux in France, depict the hunter myth, while the Venus figurines discovered across Eurasia since the middle of the nineteenth century, depict the Goddess. Whereas the Goddess myth represents the instinct for connection, the hunter myth represents the instinct to survive through separation—separation of the hunter from the animal he kills, and the separating act of cutting flesh from body. The goddess myth is all encompassing. It contains the cycle of life and death, while the hunter causes death in order to secure life for himself. The Goddess myth functions out of eternity, the hunter myth out of the necessitudes of life and linear time. The Goddess represents existence as a whole, while the hunter stands for the need to survive *inside* of existence. The Goddess connects; the hunter separates.

In terms of the relationship between ego and Self, the Goddess myth corresponds to the Self's perspective, while the hunter myth corresponds to the ego's perspective. As we have seen, in an ego-weak world such as the Paleolithic, humans *felt* reality internally. In other words, without a strong ego to enforce a psychic apartness from the outer world, the human psyche and the world interpenetrated each other.

Like the hunter, the ego affirms its existence by means of separation. The hunter must coldly detach himself from his target both to hunt and to kill it. In the same way, the ego detaches itself from the outer world in order to distinguish object from subject, inner from outer, existence from non-existence, linear time from eternity. On the other hand, the Self, like the Goddess, is non-dual. It is neither one nor many because the one and the many necessarily exclude the other. The non-dual nature of the Self allows it to be all the varying things and different creatures of the phenomenal world without ceasing to be itself. And as the Self contains the ego—since the ego is a projection of the Self—so the myth of the Goddess contains the myth of the hunter:

> "In the Mother Goddess story, the human hunter and the animals that are hunted are both contained in one vision (that of the Goddess). There is a continuum of relationship in which both hunter and hunted participate, so that the myth of the hunter is ultimately included in the myth of the Goddess...the Goddess myth contains the hunter myth, but the hunter myth cannot contain the Goddess myth."[3]

For the Goddess and for the Self, life and death "are recognized as phases of an eternal process," whereas for the isolated hunter and the lone ego, "death becomes final, and our experience of life tragic."[4]

The metaphysics of these two myths form the undercurrent of all subsequent ages of mythology. The myth of the hunter manifests as "the hero" in the Bronze and Iron ages and, in the Renaissance, as the "self-made man." In the modern era, we see the hunter manifest in the Wall Street tycoon, a self-proclaimed master of the universe, who eats what he kills. The myth of the Goddess remained prominent throughout the Neolithic Era, manifesting as various fertility goddesses, but then fell underground at the onset of the historic period, taking up secondary positions as Eve, Sophia, Hera, Demeter, Artemis, Persephone, and the Christian Mary. Despite its fall underground, the Goddess myth is clearly alive and well, having resurfaced in recent centuries. Examples of this include the official recognition of the Virgin Mary as Queen of Heaven by Pope Pius XII, the three feminist waves of the twentieth century, the discovery of the unconscious by depth psychologists, and the shift in physics from an atomically disparate view of reality (Cartesian-Newtonian) to an interconnected, synchronistic, quantum web (quantum mechanics).

By the historical period (3500 BC), the interplay between these two myths evolved into the Goddess rescuing the hunter in the form of her son or her lover (sometimes a daughter) from the underworld. The child is separated from the Goddess and dies, or falls permanently asleep, at which point the Goddess descends into the underworld to resurrect or awaken him or her.

In one of Sumer's myths, Nammu, the primordial goddess of the ocean, awakens her son Enki, who is asleep in the underworld. In another, Innana descends into the underworld and appoints her lover Dumuzi to reside there in her place. In Babylonia, Ishtar awakens her son-lover Tammuz from the underworld and brings him up into the light. For the Greeks, Hades carries off Persephone and marries her in the darkness of Hell; only when she is returned to Demeter, her mourning mother, can spring return to Earth and corn grow again. The Virgin Mary miraculously conceives Christ, who is later executed, descends into Hell for three days, and is resurrected. In Egypt, Isis loses Osiris when he his killed and dismembered by Seth. Isis must put his body back together to ensure the spring season and new life.

The theme of dismemberment is common across world mythology because it represents the dividing of the Self into multitudes and egos. In psychological terms, the ego (son/

consort) parts from the Self (Mother Goddess or Father) into linear time and is then reunited with the Self in eternity upon its temporal death. The Goddess-hunter mythic cycle also makes sense when expressed in psychological terms in reverse: the Self abandons itself to the ego, descending from eternity into a lifespan of linear time, in effect falling asleep or dying, until it reawakens or ascends back into immortal wholeness with itself upon its temporal death. The Self dies, or self-sacrifices, so that it may be born an ego. When the ego dies, the Self reclaims wholeness with itself and is reborn by reunification.

The tension between the One and the many is present in the Greek word for Eve. In the Septuagint—the Greek translation of the Torah—Eve is translated as *Zoe*. Zoe means "life," which makes sense since Eve means "mother of all living." Zoe is parent of the word "zoology," which reminds us of the unifying nature of the great Mother Goddess. Another Greek term for life is *bios*. Bios is the root word of biology, and, in contrast to the all-encompassing context of zoe, it represents life as parts, instances or categories of life such as human or ant; or mammal and reptile. Bios is life manifested in linear time and partitioned into individual lifespans, whereas zoe is life expressed within eternal time, continuous as an overarching body or process. The complementary tension between bios and zoe corresponds to the tension between the hunter and the Goddess, masculine and feminine, rational and intuitive, left brain and right brain, conscious and unconscious.

CHAPTER 6:

Paradise Lost

Better to reign in Hell than serve in Heaven!

~ Lucifer, in 'Paradise Lost'

The Paleolithic Age ended around 10,000 BC. Rather than foraging and hunting for food, humans began producing it through agriculture. As familiar to us as the activity of farming seems, it is an odd way of life that has been around for a comparatively short time. When you consider that humans hunted and gathered their dinner for over two-million years and then started farming just twelve-thousand years ago, you appreciate the gravity of this moment as a total transformation in human lifestyle and psychology—a transformation embedded in some of the first verses of Genesis. Yahweh banishes Adam and Eve from the original paradise, where they lived *with* nature to meet their needs (hunting-gathering/foraging/immediate return), to a life of agriculture, where they worked *against* nature to survive:

> "Damned be the soil on your account; with painstaking labor shall you eat from it, all the days of your life. Thorn and sting-shrub, let it spring up for you when you seek to eat the plants of the field! By the sweat of your brow shall you eat bread."[1]

The big change for humanity was time. In order for people to navigate the complex layers of settled Neolithic life, a profound sense of mental time-travel was required, and a level of planning exceeding that needed by a Paleolithic hunter-gatherer. Planting, harvesting, food processing, animal husbandry, bartering, and trading all required self-reflection and planning, and thus an orientation inside of linear time. The Neolithic mind had to fabricate the past and future more intensely than the Paleolithic mind, in order to survive and socialize. A primary sociological and psychological difference between agrarian cultures and immediate-return cultures is that in agrarian cultures you must play a specific role; you must be *somebody*—Ben the smith, Jane the weaver, Joe the miller, Seth the farmer. The role you were born into or took on in your Neolithic town was distinct from your neighbors and contributed to your individual identity.

Your identity is a knowledge of self whose shape depends on external pressure applied by interactions with other people, including strangers. Regular encounters with strangers and their ideas (statues, laws, signs, idols) only occur in densely populated, urban environments. *Identity* comes from the Latin root word *idem*, which means "sameness." *Individual* comes from the Latin *in-dividuus* (indivisible), meaning that an individual identity is an indivisible unity. An identity is only definable to the extent that it is distinguishable from other identities. Your identity is a relationship; it is a matter of differentiation from others as much as a matter of your inherent uniqueness. People who experience extended periods of isolation begin to lose their sanity because there are no other identities to mold theirs into a socially sanctioned shape. If you were the last person on Earth, against whom would you measure and define your personality? Who would you be? Who would remind you of your name?

When the last surviving member of the American-Indian Yani culture was asked his name, he replied that he had none because it was forbidden in Yani culture to utter it. Your name, he insisted, could only be said by someone else. Without any of his people left to name him, he was nobody. The taboo of saying one's own name is connected to a deep truth: it is a guard against forgetting who you *really* are. A society that forgets this truth does so at the cost of its sanity. For it is necessary to play a role in society with the implicit knowledge that is a *just* a role, that Ben the smith or Joe the miller is just a label, a façade of the Self.

Language brings reality into existence outside of you, but it is just as true to say that language brings *you* into existence within reality. The Sanskrit word for reality is *nama-rupa*, literally "name-form," or "named form." The act of naming transubstantiates form into *maya*[i], which in Sanskrit means "illusion" and is derived from another Sanskrit word, *matr*, which means to measure. Matr is the root of the Greco-Latin words "matter, material, meter, matrix, ma," and "mother." Naming is therefore an act of measuring reality. We bring existence and each other into being by measuring reality's form. We are subconsciously aware of this when we ask someone, "What is your name?" In other words, "What do I call your form?" or "How do I *measure* your form?"

Your name differentiates between a foreground (you) and a background (not you). It etches you-ness out of reality and includes your personality, which comes from the Latin word *persona*, which means "mask" or "character." Your ego is one of many characters or masks of the Self, called into being by other egos using your name. And you call their ego into being by invoking their name. By naming each other, we make each other conscious. Think of a world in which you were the last person on earth, similar to the Yani tribesman. Who would call you by your name? What would you become without people regularly calling you by your name, constantly reminding you of who you are or who you *think* you are?

---

[i] *Maya* was the name of the Buddha's mother.

Naming tears pieces of reality out of its original wholeness; it is simultaneously an act of dismemberment and an act of creation. We carve each other from the background of the web of Being through naming, thereby creating and participating in a shared, ultra-complex, symbolic web of meaning that we call reality. We pay for awareness of this grand illusion with the experience of death, which is ultimately no more than a return from the ego's specific and differentiated point of consciousness to the Self's general and undifferentiated state of unconsciousness.

Ego-consciousness—a strong sense of differentiation from others—is a constantly reinforced, psychological precondition *and* byproduct of living in an urban environment, anything from villages to towns to cities. The Neolithic Age supplied the basic, psychological ingredients of ego for the historic period. For the Modern Period, today's urban environments do likewise, but to a greater degree. The extent of ego-Self separation increases with the sophistication and scale of the civilization in which the ego is incubated.

Agriculture underlies civilization. Farming made people stationary because, unlike herds, crops don't move. Not only does intensive farming require a sedentary population—it also demands planning for an unprecedented phenomenon: food surplus. Surplus leads to population explosions, which in turn necessitate urbanization and collective social management systems, like governments.

On the other hand, typical hunter-gatherers do not remain in the same spot for more than a few days. If they stay too long in one place, they exhaust available food sources and risk starvation. And because they don't farm, they don't need to plan for planting, harvests, or food surplus. In fact, long-term food surplus is a rare luxury for a typical hunter-gatherer. Because of this, they do not have to figure out how to organize and manage large numbers of people, because their population size is constrained by what they can immediately collect from their environment. And since the total number of individuals in any hunter-gatherer group rarely exceeds a few dozen, there is no cultural pressure to hoard property, draw up laws, invent currency, or establish complex bureaucracies.

Farmers, on the other hand, can and do have more children because they squeeze the accessible energy out of their environments by means of intense cultivation. Due to this mode of food production, farmers risk overusing land, which leads to soil depletion, flash flooding, and desertification. This kind of ecological recklessness causes the regular collapse of civilization, a pattern that has plagued humanity ever since we settled into towns.[2] Sprawling towns and cities are spatial responses to runaway population explosions that occur only in agricultural and industrial societies.

CHAPTER 7:

High Hopes for Prehistoric Utopias

Prehistory is not only a period of time, but also a state of mind, a vision of the world and of humanity.

~ Mircea Eliade

Farming societies established themselves all over the world from 10,000 BC to 4,000 BC. Despite separation in both space and time, all Neolithic societies were underlaid with a shared cultural web devoted to the Mother Goddess. Cultures as far apart as Egypt, Southern Anatolia, Mesopotamia, the Indus Valley, and the Far East were replete with her image and representation in the form of carved ivory and stone figurines.[1] Her prominence likely reached even as far as Ireland.

When the Celts landed on the shores of Ireland around 500 BC, they encountered a set of Neolithic inhabitants who had been living there for at least a few thousand years. The Celtic migrants subjugated them and encased their memory in Irish lore.[i] They remembered these mysterious Neolithic people as the

[i] Both the Irish language and mythology remain largely intact today because of the enthusiastic efforts of Irish monks. After Christianity and literacy took over Ireland in the fifth century AD, Irish monks wrote down their ancient oral traditions. One of the unique aspects of Irish mythology is the central roles played by female characters. You would be hard-pressed to find active, female characters in any other contemporary epic. The women of Homer and Virgil are passive, peripheral, absent, or disposable. In part because Roman legions never set foot on Ireland's shores, Irish is one of the only remaining, original Indo-European languages and one of the oldest of the 6,500 that exist today globally. Almost all of Europe's other languages were transformed by Latin. Compared to its contemporaries (*Iliad*, *Aenid*, or *Torah*), where women almost universally play passive, peripheral and dispensable roles, ancient Irish epics contain larger-than-life, female characters such as Maeve, or goddesses like Brigid, whose forceful personalities keep them at the center of stories and in control of their own destinies. One need only catalogue some of the differences between Irish Roman Catholicism and Roman Catholicism in general, to consider that the Iron Age Celts may very well have absorbed and sustained the matrifocal sensibility of their Neolithic predecessors.

Tua De Danaan, or *People of the Goddess Danu* and imaged them as the popularly known fairies and leprechauns. Not a great deal is known about them, but we do know they built the beautifully carved tumuli and massive burial mounds still visible across the Emerald Isle today. These magnificent monoliths preceded the Great Pyramids of Giza and probably even Stonehenge. It is still not understood how, using the technology of their day, the Neolithic builders moved the tons of requisite earth and stone into place. But if you visit the Newgrange Barrows north of the River Boyne today, you may notice that their internal layout resembles a womb, a suggestion that Mother Goddess worship stretched all the way to Northern and Western Europe as well.

Some argue that, as a rule, the Mother Goddess-worshipping Neolithic societies were peaceful and valued social equity. Based on the layout of a few major Neolithic towns that we know of, such as Catal Huyuk, we can make some inferences about the social climate of the age. Catal Huyuk was established in Anatolia (modern-day Turkey) around 8500 BC and at its peak contained a population of about ten thousand. Its layout was unique by ancient standards. There were no grand, public buildings like Ziggurats or palaces which would indicate the presence of a dominating, bureaucratic rulership. No streets existed, and the settlement itself resembled a gigantic piece of honeycomb with dwellings adjoined in a hive-like superstructure. Archaeological evidence indicates that men and women ate the same foods, and nonbiological relatives were routinely buried underneath dwellings, suggesting social seamlessness and an extended familial connectedness in which the certainty of paternal lines was unimportant. Surprisingly, no palisades or defensive walls were built around the town, suggesting that war was the exception rather than the rule during the Neolithic Era.

But this would all come to an end when the invasions started. The Celtic invasions of Ireland occurred at the tail end of a broader migratory movement of warrior nomads who emerged out of the Pontic-Caspian steppes sometime around 4000 BC. These nomads, now known as the Aryans or Indo-Europeans, swept west into Europe, south into the Near East (Turkey, Syria, Palestine) and Middle East, and east into India and the steppes of Central Asia over the course of about four-thousand years. The first hints of this massive migration were discovered as early as the sixteenth century AD.

As European minds made contact with the East during the Renaissance, they were struck by surprising, fundamental similarities between Latin and Greek with Sanskrit, one of the oldest languages of the Far East. Near the end of the eighteenth century, a philologist named William Jones proposed the existence of a distant parent language of the Indus and European regions that he called Indo-European. Scholars now trace the origins of many language families including Balto-Slavic (Russian, Lithuanian, Serbian, Polish, Czech, etc.) Hellenic (Greek), Italic (Latin), Celtic (Irish, Cornish, Welsh etc), Germanic (English, German, Swedish, Norwegian, Dutch, etc.), Albanian, Armenian, Iranian (and its many variations and descendants, such as Kurdish), Sanskrit, and Hindi to an ultimate parent language called Proto-Indo-European or PIE. Some believe that the nomadic waves of Indo-Europeans ruptured the Neolithic societies they encountered.

Unlike the sedentary, matrifocal, peaceful Neoliths, the steppe nomads were hyper-mobile, patriarchal, and violent, or so the narrative goes. By the fourth and third millenniums BC, the steppe nomads had domesticated the horse, invented the spoked wheel along with the war chariot, and worshipped a Sky-Father called "Diespiter," which their Greek descendants would call *Zeu Piter* or "Father Zeus" and their Roman descendants *Jupiter.* Indo-Europeans were a warrior cult whose culture was based on the heroic code. They would become the Celts, the Germanics, the Latins (Romans), the Mycenaeans (Greeks), the Slavs, the Armenians, the Hittites, the Pontics, the Iranians, and the

Indians (Vedics). That the Indo-European migration into India occasioned the historical appearance of the caste system is not coincidental. It may be that the bottom rung of the caste system, the untouchables, were the remnants of the original, Neolithic people that the invaders subjugated. The domineering steppe folk were a group of hardened, linguistically diverse nomads whose societal structure introduced, enforced, and at least set the foundation for social hierarchy and male domination in history.

Cultural historian Riane Eisler argued that the social style of the Neolithic, a style of equal partnership between men and women underpinned by worship of the Great Mother Goddess, was usurped by the Indo-European "dominator" style. This style is characterized by male social dominance, misogyny, violence, and a general set of values and institutions that normalizes such behavior. The mythological transition from Earth Mother to Sky Father, Eisler believes, reflects a fundamental social shift from *partnership* to *dominator*, that occasioned the end of the prehistoric Neolithic Era and ushered in the Bronze Age, which marked the beginning of recorded history. By the third millennium BC, the dominator style had been internalized throughout the earliest historic civilizations, including the Sumerians, the Egyptians, and the Vedics.

In virtually all historic societies from then on in Europe, with the possible exception of Crete[ii], kings and priests ruled, women lost social status, wives became obedient and subservient to their husbands, and a subjugated underclass took on most of the agricultural and infrastructural labor. Semitic nomads like the Akkadians, Babylonians, and Hebrews, arguably distantly related to the nomads of the Caspian steppes, also worshipped sky and mountain gods and invariably acted out the dominator

[ii] Perhaps because of its isolation, Crete's Neolithic culture (Minoa) was preserved until 1500 BC. The Minoans left behind figurines (like the snake goddess) and pottery displaying evidence of bull worship, connecting them to the Neolithic civilizations of the Near East (like Catal Huyuk). Either due to volcanic explosion or invasion by the Mycenaeans, the Minoan civilization disappeared around 1500 BC and with it possibly the last remaining Goddess culture of Old Europe.

style. Semitic or Indo-European, these invading waves of nomadic warriors toppled the Mother Goddess and conquered her peaceful, Neolithic communitarians.

But the idea that Neolithic humans lived in some peaceful, agrarian paradise sounds wishfully utopian. One only has to visit the remnants of Neolithic megalithic structures today and wonder how their huge rocks were dragged onsite and put into place. It seems naïve to imagine some egalitarian society blissfully working as one to move thousands of tons of rock and materials dozens of miles uphill and then assemble it as a team. Like the pyramids of Giza and Mesoamerica, it is more likely that an unfortunate class of human bodies was thrown at these projects until completion. These Neolithic societies were united in their worship of a Mother Goddess, but the extent to which her divine love perpetuated social partnership and equality throughout her societies is an open question.

Did her prehistoric cultures really disappear because of marauding misogynists on horseback? No one knows exactly what happened to the Neoliths at the prehistoric-historic juncture. Some believe that they succumbed to climate change and ecological disaster, that many of the Neolithic agrarians exhausted their land, cut down too many trees, and could no longer sustain their populations. Maybe the Indo-Europeans interbred with, rather than conquered, the settled, agrarian societies they encountered.[2] Rather than being vanquished by the blades of Aryan nomads, maybe the Mother Goddess was abstracted away by the writing stylus of civilized scribes. In other words, perhaps the cognitive effects of literacy psychologically shifted civilization away from a holistic, right-brained, egalitarian, feminine-revering outlook to a particularized, left-brained, individualistic, masculine-dominating worldview.

In a certain sense, Neolithic societies never went away. The subsequent Bronze Age civilizations inherited much from them. Whatever the case may be, the Indo-European waves and the resulting cultural zigzag from feminine to masculine, from prehistory to history, coincided with the appearance of the mythic-hero archetype. The appearance of the hero symbolizes ego-consciousness and announces the beginning of collective, historic self-reflection. This is to say that the cosmos woke up at the advent of man's recorded history.

CHAPTER 8:

The Hero and the Dragon

The dragon represents the unseen, unknown aspects of life and consciousness, and the hero's task is to confront and overcome these unconscious powers.

~ Joseph Campbell

The hero is central to all major epics and myths of the world. The hero's journey is a circular trip in which he leaves home, encounters trials and dangerous foes that he must overcome to reach a goal, and then returns home, transformed. His goal is often a meeting with the divine, or overcoming death, or attainment of some life-giving object (such as the elixir of life or the golden fleece). Although the hero's goal is to gain something, it always turns out, as Joseph Campbell tells us, that his "perilous journey was a labor not of attainment but of re-attainment, not discovery but rediscovery."[1] The first epic heroes were Gilgamesh, King of Uruk, and Sargon of Akkadia. For Homer, his heroes were Achilles and Odysseus. For Virgil it was Aeneas, founder of Rome. Gautama Buddha, Muhammad, and Jesus all fit the archetype of the cosmic hero.

Archetypes fulfill a personal and collective role. The personal function of the hero archetype is the urge toward individuation, which means that the hero is a precursor to the development of mature ego-hood. The hero has the energy we need to grow up. It propels the ego out of its containment within the collective unconscious, mythically seen as the battle with the unbeatable foe, often depicted in the West as a powerful, feminine force like a dragon, the sea, or the Goddess herself. While the hero's energy can break the ego free of the unconscious, if left unchecked the archetype can also lead the ego into trouble. The danger of the hero, as with any archetype, is possession. For the person must experience a *psychological* death—the hero must be sacrificed—so that their ego individuates. But one who is fully possessed by the hero will also ensure a physical, temporal death by eventually running themselves and those around them into ruin.

An example of possession by the heroic principle is the Germanic berserkers. They fought with such reckless abandon they were known to fell both friend and foe during battle. Possessed unconsciously by the hero, corporate executives take the uncalculated risk, trampling their employees and running their organizations into the ground. In his inflated heroic state, Roman Emperor Caligula presumed himself to be the god Jove, exacted needless cruelty on his own people, and was later assassinated by his own bodyguards.

One of the eerier things about the hero myth is the fact that we find it everywhere. It is present in virtually all cultures, including that of the Hebrews, Babylonians, Persians, Greeks, Egyptians, Indians, Germans, and Irish, to name a few.[2] There are a number of elements common to this myth. For example, the hero is almost always the offspring of royal or divine parents. He is usually adopted, as in the cases of Moshe (Moses) and Sargon. Before the hero's birth, sages forewarn of danger to the established powers, classically a male god/king, such as Apsu, Kronos, or Pharaoh. Measures are taken to either prevent the hero's birth or to kill the hero once born. Often the child is given away to foster parents to protect him from these destructive forces.

Psychohistorically, the heroic age, the dawn of the historic period, symbolizes the cosmos's individuation into the ego, its abandonment of all-view to a point of view. God made man so that God could "taste the bitter fruit of time."[3] This was a cosmic moment of separation between the unconscious and the ego. The name of the Hebrew hero Moshe means "he who pulls out."[i] "For out of the water *meshitihu,* I pulled him" said the Egyptian princess who rescued him.[4] Water is one of the most common symbols of the collective unconscious.

The heroic action of ego separation from the unconscious is reflected in hero-dragon mythology. Upon closure of the Neolithic Age around 3500 BC, Western mythology became fixated on killing reptiles. During the war with the Titans, Zeus slays Typhon, a massive, multi-headed dragon-spawn of Gaia, an image of the Great Goddess inherited from the Neolithic Era. In the biblical Book of Isaiah, Yahweh slays the dragon who lives in the sea. In another Greek example, Perseus rescues Andromeda from the sea-dragon Cetus. According to popular Christian legend, Saint George tramples and kills the dragon.

In Paolo Di Dono's fifteenth-century painting of *Saint George and the Dragon,* a mounted Saint George kills a dragon leashed to a regal-looking woman near the entrance of a dark cave. What is interesting about Di Dono's rendition of this theme is that the woman does not look like the typical, princess hostage: quite the opposite. She stands erect, holding in her right hand a sash cord wrapped around the dragon's neck. Her left palm is turned upward toward the heavens as she watches Saint George pierce the dragon's eye with his lance. The dragon looks to be her pet or protector.

Although in many versions of this story the princess assists Saint George, the moment captured by Di Dono forces us to consider this question: is she being rescued or kidnapped? Saint George's heroic deed as the male "savior" emulates Yahweh's effort to separate Eve, the mother of all living, the Great Goddess of the Neolithic, from the serpent in the early verses of Genesis:

---

[i] A foreshadowing of Moshe one day pulling the Hebrews out of Egypt.

"I put enmity between you and the woman, between your seed and her seed."[5]

Like Yahweh, Saint George severs the female-dragon relationship. Similar to how Adam and Eve undergo a transformation of consciousness that catalyzes their fall from paradise, after Saint George slays the dragon and rescues the princess, the nearby villagers give up their pagan religion and convert to Christianity. Psychologically understood, the masses gained a significant enough presence of ego to cognize a monotheistic ontology. Whether rescued or separated by coercion, the feminine is pulled out of its partnership with the instinctual, into relationship with the masculine, which is to say that it is brought out of the unconscious above the line of consciousness. The dragon-slaying quest represents man's separation from his instincts, a separation from the shared mind of nature.

One jarring version of the hero-dragon myth is the Babylonian epic known as the *Enuma Elish* (1750 BC), which tells the heroic tale of the god Marduk killing and dismembering the sea-dragon goddess, Tiamat. Earlier Sumerian myths depict a heroic god slaying a dragon, but none of them match the violence and ferocity of the Babylonian creation epic. Perhaps this is because the *Enuma Elish* was conceived toward the end of the Bronze Age, an increasingly violent and chaotic period in which ancient civilization would eventually implode. This is known as the Bronze Age Collapse.

Virtually all ancient Bronze Age civilizations—including the Assyrians, the Babylonians, the Canaanites, the Mitanni, the Cypriots, the Hittites, the Trojans, the Minoans, and the Mycenaeans (predecessors to the Greeks)—fell simultaneously for reasons ranging from war to natural disasters like famine, drought, and volcanic eruptions. The sole survivor was mighty Egypt, though it emerged from the chaos a shell of its former self and never fully recovered. This mass-collapse event heralded a darkened age of social turmoil, lawlessness, and illiteracy known as the Iron Age (1250–600 BC). The *Enuma Elish* captured the collective mind and heart of the proto-West during this time and set the foundation for the new wave of Judaic religions that would gradually take over the West over the next two-thousand years.

In typical primordial, mythic fashion, the *Enuma Elish* starts with Apsu, the primordial father, planning to kill his children. The original mother, Tiamat, tries to persuade him otherwise, but Apsu proceeds with his plan on counsel from his advisor, Mummu.[ii] When the younger gods become aware of Apsu's plot, one of them (called Ea) kills Apsu instead, copulates with his wife Damkina over the cosmic father's corpse, and creates Marduk, who becomes king of the Babylonian gods.[iii] In the meantime, Ea's older brother Anu creates a great wind that provokes the waters of the primordial mother, Tiamat, turning her into an angry sea-dragon. In her dragon form, Tiamat births eleven sea-serpent gods to aid her in battle against the younger gods. She takes one of them, Kingu, as her lover.

Tiamat battles Marduk. As Tiamat opens her mouth to devour him, Marduk drives the Evil Wind into her belly and shoots an arrow into it causing it to explode. Marduk steps onto Tiamat's wounded form, crushes her skull with his mace, cuts up her body, and lays out its pieces, stretching them out to make the sky, earth, rivers and mountains of the world. The division of pieces of the Great Mother into the material of the earth (*mother* as we noted is connected to the word *matter*) can be understood as the ego awakening by the division of the world into separate objects and events. This violent gesture symbolizes the application of order, associated with a heavenly Father and light, onto chaos, associated with Mother Earth and darkness.

---

ii Mummu comes from the Sumerian word "umun" which means "knowledge" making it related to *Logos*.

iii This story mirrors Zeus usurping Kronos after the titan attempts to eat the Olympians.

After dismembering the primordial Goddess, Marduk tells his father Ea that he will create "a savage, 'man' shall be his name."[6] Ea advises Marduk to sacrifice Kingu as a scapegoat for the rebellion against the old gods and use his blood to make man. Marduk and Ea tie up Kingu, impose the guilt of the rebellion on him, open his veins, and create man out of his blood.

Kingu corresponds to the serpent in Eden. Like Kingu, the snake is a reptilian companion to the central feminine figure (Tiamat/Eve) and is then punished by the creator. Like Kingu, the serpent in Genesis bears culpability for man's rebellion, his sin[iv] of disobeying Yahweh by eating the forbidden fruit of the Tree of Knowledge of Good and Evil, precipitating man's fall out of unconscious bliss into ego-awareness.

By the beginning of the Iron Age, the descent into linear time out of eternity is no longer collectively regarded as part of a circular pattern in which a Goddess loses and then recollects her son or daughter, but is seen instead as a tragic, cosmic error—a usurping or robbery of sorts. Someone needed to be held responsible. Kingu's forced sacrifice expunges the collective guilt of the rebel gods and supplies the blood to create man, thereby connecting guilt with man's essential substance. It is difficult to miss Kingu's anticipation of Christ, son of a divine mother who is sacrificed and sheds his blood for the redemption of man's great sin.

The *Enuma Elish* is a radical departure from the tone and sensibility of the Paleolithic, Neolithic, and early Bronze Age mythology. The Goddess no longer births Heaven and Earth from her life-giving form, but instead is reimagined as a ferocious dragon who must be defeated. No rescue of an eternally sleeping son by the Great Mother occurs anymore; rather, the mother is slain and her son-lover executed by a male god who then takes

[iv] Saint Augustine of Hippo interpreted this guilt as Original Sin, washed away by the Roman Catholic sacrament of Baptism. "Sin" means to miss the target. Baptism symbolically allows the person to find their way back to original wholeness prior to man's sin of deviation into ego-consciousness.

command of creation. The world is no longer a living organism continuous with the body of the Goddess, as an inside in an already greater inside; it is now *made* with pieces of her dead body from the *outside* by the conscious will of a god. Marduk's dismemberment of Tiamat and the laying out of her body as the world, represents the shift from humanity's containment within nature to its confrontation with and desire to control it. The *Enuma Elish* is a forerunner to modern, scientific materialism and the troubling, modern view of nature as inert and dead and therefore exploitable and expendable.

This is the myth out of which the proto-Western psyche emerges. It materialized into what would become the heart of Zoroastrianism, Judaism, Christianity, and Islam. It would become, in a way, a Western metaphysic, for this myth cemented (and reflected) the implicit opposition forming in the Western mind between order and chaos, mind and body (or mind and matter), spirit and nature,[7] or, expressed in modern, scientific, materialistic terms: the left and right brains. At this point in history, Mircea Eliade notes, "darkness is no longer valorized as a necessary phase in cosmic life…it is opposed to life, to forms, and to intelligence."[8] The Babylonian epic/myth exposes the source of Western man's distrust of chaos, his need to dominate nature, and his unexamined guilt about his own existence. Human life becomes something to be ashamed of—or, expressed in its most optimistic terms by modern scientism: a cosmic accident.

The *Enuma Elish* shows the beginning of a new kind of worldview, one in which active, conscious energies contest the inert energies of the unconscious. The masculine principles of light, mind, and order become associated with "good" and subordinate the feminine principles of darkness, body, matter, and chaos, which now equate with "evil."[9] Not until the beginning of the historic period do we see the birth of religions in which mind has been separated from matter, spirit from body, "thinking from feeling, intellect from intuition, reason from instinct" and time from eternity.[10] At this historical moment, in an unconscious process of birthing, the proto-Western psyche shifts from a right-brain perspective (feeling existence as a concrete whole unified with the Great Mother) to a left-brain perspective (seeing existence as the resulting effect of a conscious, male, causal force).

PART II:
AFTER THE FALL

CHAPTER 9:

A Quantum Leap of Self-Consciousness

The invention of writing and the recording of history mark the birth of human self-reflection and self-awareness.

~ Walter J. Ong

In 3,500 BC, about two-thousand years before the *Enuma Elish* was carved into clay tablets, human history entered the Bronze Age. So-called because of the invention of a tin-copper alloy that greatly improved the effectiveness of the plow and sword, the Bronze Age marks a milestone of consciousness. This is the beginning of recorded history.

Whereas the Neolithic Period left us no written records of religious pantheons, royal genealogies, or epics of heroes, we now see recorded for the first time in history the names of individuals and deities and a general fascination with their personalities, motivations, objectives, and attitudes. The first story ever written down, the *Epic of Gilgamesh,* comes out of the Bronze Age. The reason for this is not simply because the technology of writing was invented, that people finally found a way to memorialize names, places, ideas, and stories. The prehistoric Neoliths were already sophisticated artists, sculptors, smiths, and builders. Had they needed to externalize memory in such a specialized way, they would have done so.[i]

The fact that we see the very first appearance of stories and names of kings and deities in the Bronze Age has to do with the astonishing wave of self-reflectiveness rippling across civilized humanity, an intensifying waking up of the individual to itself inside of time. And the rise of this individuality directly corresponds to the rise of literacy because writing, more than oral language, objectifies reality for a person, abstractly crystallizing the external world in a psychic stasis field of language. Writing was and probably still is the most catalytic invention of human history, for it is the primary vehicle by which the Self birthed ego-consciousness.

Writing had the effect of exteriorizing the human mind in a way that had never been done before. In a temple or warehouse within the three-hundred-acre megalopolis of Uruk a little over five-thousand years ago, a hand carved the first written word onto a small, clay tablet in a style called cuneiform. At first, cuneiform was pictographic (right-brained). Images of mounds meant mountains, a six-pointed star represented a god, a *V* with a slit down its middle signified Woman. But the need for richer, more dynamic communication arose as populations ballooned and human settlements grew in complexity due to better farming technology and techniques. The Bronze Age thus saw towns become cities, cities turn into city-states, and city-states constellate into empires.

Writing allowed urban systems to scale in size and complexity, enabling both intracity and intercity cohesion. The fact that the world's first empire was a Bronze Age phenomenon has as much to do with the dawn of literacy as it does with advancements in weaponry and farming technology. Without applications of

---

[i] Prehistoric Old Europe may have even invented a kind of protoscript. See Marija Gimbutas, *The Goddesses and Gods of Old Europe: 6500 – 3500 BC Myths and Cult Images* (Los Angeles: University of California Press, 1974), page 17.

writing such as currency and laws, an emperor could not extend rule from a central location across far-flung territories and expect to administrate them efficiently and cohesively.

With the Bronze Age, we also see for the first time evidence of people divided up into classes and specialized by function and occupation. Unlike a hunter-gatherer who might be able to perform all the needed functions of their group at any one time, an urbanite performs a specialized job and falls into a social class. Specialization is a symptom of an ego-conscious society. As more people migrated into urban centers to perform specific jobs, direct contact with nature waned. Monumental architecture (ziggurats and pyramids) appeared. Elaborate forms of abstraction—mathematics, astronomy, and writing—arose within the precincts of these structures, consciously integrating human affairs with the cosmic pattern of the heavens.

If you left our building in Uruk and toured the lush banks of the Euphrates River, you would find it dotted with cities remarkably similar to Uruk in culture and organization, though lesser in scale. Each city-state belonged to Sumer, which by the end of the fourth millennium BC had come to dominate Mesopotamia.

The Sumerians were practical, business-minded folk. They applied the magic of the written word toward matters like accounting and trading. The earliest cuneiform tablets were used for trading sheep for barley, counting surplus in a grain warehouse, or tallying a farmer's debts. The Sumerians credited their goddess Nisaba, the deity of grain and storage, for gifting them cuneiform.[1] Another one of their gods, Ninurta, authored a farming manual complete with information on how to protect fields from birds and mice.

The civilizations of the Nile and Indus valleys had extensive trade links with Sumer and would at times fall under its dominion. Unlike the Sumerians who used literacy to count, trade, and tally, these communities generally reserved literacy for matters of the divine. The Egyptians would invent their own pictographic version of literacy called "hieroglyphics" some five-hundred years after cuneiform appeared.

Roaming the mountains and desert outskirts of Uruk and its sister cities were illiterate, Semitic nomads known as Amorites. The Amorites and Sumerians regarded each other with a mixture of fear and curiosity. While the civilized Sumerians looked down their noses at the savage, tent-dwelling outsiders, we can imagine the nomads in turn regarding the Sumerians as arrogant and soft, unworthy of their riches, and deluded by their superior pretensions. By 2400 BC, a powerful group of Amorites known as the Akkadians invaded from the north and conquered the Sumerians.

The Akkadians immediately saw the genius of cuneiform. It would take them about a century to modify it to accommodate their language. Cuneiform, like hieroglyphics, was originally pictographic, made up mostly of ideograms: images that directly corresponded to an object or action. The Akkadians had to convert cuneiform's characters into phonograms to transliterate the syllables of their language into written form.[2] With the Akkadian modification, a cuneiform character could now represent the image of an actual thing in the world *and* the sound of a word. The Akkadians invented something brilliant: phonetic writing. Phonetics opened literacy to increased levels of abstraction. These were desperately needed, since the earliest forms of writing, cuneiform and hieroglyphics, had become cumbersome and unwieldy, comprising six-hundred to seven-hundred symbols[ii], respectively.[3] As such, each took a lifetime to master, so only an elite, dedicated class of scribes—normally a priesthood—could be literate.

A sign representing the sound of a word whose meaning is specific to a culture's language, is more abstract (and thus

ii By comparison, an alphabet, invented some two-thousand years later, typically contains about thirty symbols.

less accessible to outsiders) than a universal image of a star, a woman, or mountains. It would not be long before the Akkadians invented words that had absolutely no correlate in concrete reality—words like *justice* or *honor.* And by 2300 BC, in order to improve the accessibility of its meaning, the Akkadians began to write cuneiform in the linear flow of left-to-right. The linear-oriented left brain was being emphasized in a way like never before.

When Akkadian rule declined toward the end of the third millennium BC, another set of Semites from the south, known as the Babylonians, filled the power vacuum. The well-known city of Babylon originated in southern Sumer and is known for its famous ruler Hammurabi, who asserted control over greater Sumer during the eighteenth century BC. The utility and power of literacy were not lost on the Babylonians, either. Much like how the Akkadians transliterated their language into cuneiform, the Babylonians transcribed their model of human behavior into cuneiform that we know as Hammurabi's code.[iii]

On the surface, a law is enabled by writing. But on a deeper level, laws are unique, abstract constructs of societies that emphasize the individual. Laws oppose feminine principles of spontaneity and intuition which underlie the social consciousness of tribal cultures. Laws promote ego-consciousness. Leonard Shlain explains it well:

> "This peculiar pairing of events—the ascendancy of written laws and the decline of feminine power—can be traced to a feature unique to writing...For the [preliterate], conduct is regulated by taboos that are acknowledged by everyone in the tribe. Elders and shamans pass down these conventions through oral teaching. Tribal mores discourage individuality;

iii Hammurabi's famous law code was one of the earliest, but not the first, examples of written law. We find earlier instances of Sumerian laws stretching back into the third millennium BC.

> everyone is inextricably enmeshed in the community at large, and in general, violating a taboo brings misfortune on everyone. Breaking a *law*, however, singles out an individual. This significant distinction encourages individuality and ego development in literate societies. Customs organically grow with the maturing of a community; laws press down upon the people and can be initiated and manipulated by a privileged literate elite."[4]

Literacy was not only an administrative and economic tool for towns to mushroom into sophisticated cities, but it also worked to cut society's collective psyche into particulates called egos. Alan Watts pointed out that "governments and states have to exist when people have no inner feeling of their solidarity with others, when human society is nothing more than an abstract term for a collection of individuals—divided from each other because each one is divided from himself."[5] Literacy, and by extension rule of law, atomize societies into individuals by demystifying and objectifying reality. This psychologically separates the people from the web of consciousness that interconnects reality.

The birth of *I* coincided with the first kings, for the king represents the outstanding person, the supreme individual. The first kings arose alongside the invention of literacy. The king is the initial representation of the Self's successful individuation in recorded history. Erich Neumann comments on this:

"Historically, the Great Individual is most accessible to us in the role of the god-king and, later, the king. The earliest cuneiform pictogram for "king" signifies "great man," and this was the way he was always pictured in the art of the ancient East. The Great King or the Great House, Pharaoh, is the embodiment and representative of the people."[6]

At first the king is the sole simulacrum of God. Unlike the masses, he has a name emblazoned in stone and a personal lineage, which disclose his subjugation to linear time, for neither are conceivable without understanding one's lifespan as a separate event and one's ego as a distinct identity from the wider, human continuum. To the extent that he has become ego-conscious, the king has become conscious of the Self at his center. He has individuated. And to the extent that he has individuated, he holds the collective projection of the Self cast by the masses, who are incomplete, unconscious individuals. Because he carries this collective projection, the *imago dei,* he is treated as a divine ruler or a god-king.

But the king figure's fundamental role is to be the medium through which self-consciousness is transferred to the broader population. This is his ultimate purpose. The king conducts self-consciousness from Heaven into himself and then outward to the masses. As this process unfolds through history, the king eventually loses his divine status while the population gains individual consciousness. The king disseminates his divinity or *mana* to the masses who eat him, a symbolic process of king-sacrifice that shows up in many cultures. The consumption of Christ's divine body during the Catholic eucharistic sacrament symbolizes this process, for Christ 'the King' is the symbol of the Self and the supreme individual to the Christian West. Once the king is "eaten" by the masses, the Self emerges from within their unconscious into consciousness. The Self is no longer projected into a human figure, but is now *introjected.* That is, each individual feels themselves as a separated identity.

The king who was once divine and distant, has now become secularized and familiar. We can observe this phenomenon historically by tracing the line of the god-king figure in the ancient world to its eventual obsolescence and final displacement by the secular, strictly political leader of the modern and post-modern eras of the West. An important culmination of this process occurred in the twelfth century when English barons and clergy pressured the king of England to sign the *Magna Carta Libertatum*, the earliest of many events in the post-classical world that limited the arbitrary power of the king over the people and granted rights and protections to those beneath him.

The spread of literacy corresponds to the king's loss of divine projection. The more literate humanity, the more individualistic its people become, and the less divine their rulers seem. Across the ancient world, literacy was confined to the priests, royalty, and scribes who represented the top 1% of the population. Individuation started with the king in part because the king was one of the few literates. This is how things were for a long time. Not until the invention of the alphabet did literacy become widely accessible. In alphabetic societies, as literacy spreads, more people become self-conscious simulacrums of God. This, as Erich Neumann pointed out, "in Judaism and in somewhat modified form in Christianity was to become the basic factor in man's psychic life."[7] This makes sense when you consider that the Hebrews were the first culture to require common literacy among its people. The Jews are the People of the Book: everyone had to be able to read God's Word.

It is then no surprise then that the social ideology of the West evolved into the liberal democracy, for it sanctifies the individual and works to minimize constraints on individual freedom. There is nothing more sacred to the modern West than the individual. The individual is the seed of the Western worldview. The minds and generations of one special family fertilized this seed.

CHAPTER 10:

The Family Who Started It All

We, too, shall die without finishing what we began. That accomplishment is intergenerational may be the deepest of all Hebrew insights.

~ Thomas Cahill[1]

The family lived in Ur around 1800 BC, the southern-most city of Sumer, only a few kilometers from our dusty warehouse in Uruk where the first cuneiform symbol was carved nearly two millennia before. This is how their story begins:

> "Now these are the begettings of Terah: Terah begot Avram, Nahor, and Haran, and Haran begot Lot. Terah took Avram, his son, and Lot, son of Haran, his son's son, and Sarai, his daughter-in-law, wife of Avram his son. They set out together from Ur of the Chaldeans, to go to the land of Canaan. But when they had come as far as Harran, they settled there."[2]

Terah's family were Amorite[i]. They were the most recent in a line of generations who had abandoned their nomadic life and settled in the urban centers they once had raided. We are told by the narrator of this passage that Terah's destination is Canaan, a Semitic place of lore still known to Terah's family by oral

[i] The Sumerians generalized Semites as Amorite. It should be noted that the Hebrews distinguish themselves from Amorites, calling themselves the "Sons of Shem."

tradition. But it is with the obvious benefit of hindsight that we are told of this journey to Canaan, for the anonymous narrator wrote these words probably in or around Canaan toward the beginning of the first millennium BC. The writer was in effect recording their extended family's history, an almost unthinkable phenomenon at that time.

It is unlikely that our man Terah originally set out for Canaan. Terah was a successful craftsman who made a living selling idols of the various gods of the Sumerian pantheon. Like any proud Sumerian, Terah was a businessman. Some traditions connect him to the Babylonian elite, which if true means that he was certainly literate and that his sojourn to Harran was probably for practical reasons. Whatever the case, he died in Harran, and it would be here that his eldest son, Avram, sole inheritor of his father's estate, would encounter the Voice. This Voice, Yahweh, commanded Avram to sojourn out of Sumer: "Go you forth from your land, from your kindred, from your father's house, to the land that I will let you see."[3]

Once in the desert, Avram made a blood pact with the Voice, forfeiting the foreskin of his penis and promising the same from his male descendants: "You shall circumcise the flesh of your foreskin, so that it may serve as a sign of the covenant between me and you. At eight days old, every male among you shall be circumcised, throughout your generations."[4]

Avram and Yahweh were striking a deal. Whatever occurred between them must have been an ordeal nothing short of mystical. Afterwards Avram changes his name to *Avraham* and the name of his wife, Sarai, to *Sara* which, as Everett Fox points out, was an act that in the ancient world constituted supreme significance. One's birth name in the ancient world tied him or her to a certain fate[i], one locked up with the zodiac. Changing one's name symbolized the articulation of an entirely new

[i] You may recognize here the elements of ancient-world astrology, which attempt to decode an individual's fate by recording the precise coordinates of celestial bodies at the time of their birth.

destiny, which in effect equated to a new person and therefore a new life. Avraham's heroic journey out of Babylonian Sumer into the desert wilderness would seed the new life of the nascent West, an outlook that could only come into existence inside of a mind molded by urbanization and literacy. It is important to remember that Avraham lived within historically novel circumstances. He came from Ur, the world's first city, a human development on a scale unseen in the previous Neolithic Age.

But why at the direction of a voice in his head (presumably) would he force his household to leave the comfort and predictability of urban life for the unforgiving and unpredictable desert? At first glance, Avraham's decision to abandon urban life at the behest of a mysterious voice might seem the product of a disturbed mind. But the insane do not survive long in the desert. One needs to be wily, pragmatic, and decisive to negotiate existence there. And Avraham had no shortage of any such characteristics if the Old Testament narratives contain an essential truth to them. He negotiated deals with Canaanite elites and interacted with the Egyptian pharaoh himself. This was a powerful and wealthy desert chieftain, not a madman on a suicide mission.

Such power was not at all historically unheard of for Semitic nomads. As we have discussed, the Semitic Akkadians once ruled Sumer, and the Babylonian dynasty of Hammurabi was still in power during Avraham's life. The period during which Yosef, one of Avraham's descendants, held a position in Pharoah's court coincides with the Hyksos invasion of Egypt during the seventeenth century BC. The Hyksos were Semites from the Levant who rose to power during Avraham's lifetime and ruled over Egypt for about a century, lending historical weight to the prospect of Yosef's royal position and Avraham's regular contact with Egyptian elites.

And so it is with a sincere curiosity that we should approach the story of Avraham. Is the Voice that prompted him to leave Sumer the same voice we encounter when we dialogue with ourselves: Should I do that? Should I not do that? To whom, exactly, are we asking these questions? And who answers? In other words, who or what is my conscience? Would I even *hear* a voice that "spoke" words inside my skull if I weren't literate and didn't live in a literate society? Is there a voice subvocally speaking these words as you read them right now? Is the experience of conscience, the guide to awareness, the quintessence of the *individual,* a fully-fledged, conscious, and active microcosm of the universe? The Voice's promise to Avraham, "the land that I will let you see," was a new way of viewing the world. The promised reality was the *processive* worldview.

Time was a circle for the ancients. It had no beginning or end. To them the future was nothing more than a replaying of the past. Human beings were subject to the eternal cycle of the zodiac, their fates written in the stars. The waxing and waning of the moon, the spinning of the dome above, the cycle of the seasons, and the fertility of the Great Goddess followed a pattern that never ended. The cosmos was a wheel spinning inside of eternity, symbolized by the ouroboros, the dragon-snake eating its own tail. Humans were inextricable from the patterns of movement in the star canopy above, and so the events of their lives were predetermined, set in accordance with the action of the cosmos. This is the cyclical worldview.

But with Avraham came the processive worldview, which, as Thomas Cahill tells us:

> "...is regularly referred to in history, literature, philosophy, religion, and theology texts and regularly contrasted with its opposite: the cyclical worldview... In a cyclical world, there are neither beginnings nor ends. But for us, time has a beginning, whether it was the first words of God in the Book of Genesis, when 'in the beginning God created Heaven and Earth,' or

> the Big Bang of modern science, a concept that would not have been possible without the Jews."[5]

It is difficult to overstate the gravity of the implications of the two worldviews. The processive worldview is that time unfolds as the past, present, and future. Whereas in a cyclical worldview the future is predetermined (and thus unreal since a future that is known is already past), in a processive worldview the future is unset or at least unknown (and thus real). And if the future is unset, then my actions must matter. My choices must mean something. In a processive worldview, my choices, my will—the inner condition of a conscious individual—brings the future into existence.

In a cyclical world there are no real choices, no free will, and no real individuals. What happened will happen again. Here human events are a lesser part of a greater macrocosm, trapped in sync with the cosmos and the turning wheel of the zodiac. But in a processive world, human events lie outside the overarching pattern of the cosmos, within a narrative timeline called "history." If the future is set, then history ends, and in this kind of world there is no free will in any real sense of those words. Myths recur cyclically, while history moves forward into an open-ended future. Individuals do not exist in myth: archetypes do. Individuals only exist in history, for a condition of being an individual is seeing oneself historically.

CHAPTER 11:

Ego:God

In the Self the ego knows itself immortal, and in itself mortal; the connection between the two comes out in the Talmudic saying 'Man and God are twins.'

~ *Erich Neumann*[1]

The processive worldview accompanies the historical coincidence of the ego and monotheism. Although the Hebrews were not alone in experimenting with monotheism, they are the only ones who successfully maintained it inside of a world soaked in polytheism. After expelling the Hyksos from the Nile Valley in the seventeenth century BC, the Egyptians adopted a kind of pseudo-monotheism, elevating the god Amon above other gods by decree of Thutmose III. One century later, this experiment would culminate with Amenhotep IV, also known as Akhenaton, who was widely considered the world's first monotheist. He singlehandedly reformed Egyptian religion by focusing worship exclusively onto one god, Aton. After Akhenaton's death, however, the Egyptians reverted to polytheism.

The Abrahamic religions are in a sense psychohistorical byproducts of ego-centricity. Subordinating the Great Goddess and the serpent, who represent the shared, boundless mind of nature, was a matter of self-preservation for Yahweh. A shared mind is an irreconcilable state of mind to the ego because psychic boundaries are absolutely necessary for ego-definition.

A boundless state of collective mind is unconscious and must "be guarded against," as Job noted, because it *necessarily* obliterates ego. This is why one of Yahweh's first orders of business after laying out the structure of the universe was to put distance between the serpent and humanity. Yahweh was right to fear the irrational and preconscious state of human cognition because it was intuited, immediate, concrete, pictographic, right-brained, and incapable of conceiving him; for Yahweh, being invisible, unimaginable, omnipresent, and omni-temporal, is the ultimate left-brain abstraction.

The Hebrews probably adopted monotheism gradually. Originally, Avraham was almost certainly a polytheist. Yahweh may have started out as a household god, or "shapshus," carried as one of a few amulets in Avraham's tunic. Yahweh's voice became more urgent, regular, and singular to Avraham, yes, but to say that Avraham began as or even became an orthodox monotheist in his life would be to ignore the context of his culture and time.[2] The Voice Avraham heard was of a god who later admitted to Moshe at Mount Sinai a jealousy toward others of his kind: "You shall have no other gods besides me." The first commandment presumes that other gods exist, and the Hebrews themselves, having just fled the polytheistic, image-laden land of Egypt, were caught somewhere between polytheism and monotheism.

But any sort of wavering was unacceptable to Yahweh. His identity and nature depended on a particular kind of mind: a unified, *individuated* mind specializing in abstraction. Like a written law, Yahweh is everywhere yet nowhere, transcending both space and time. Like a thought or word, he does not inhabit a spatial domain in the concrete world. He is not, like the Goddess, limited to the stuff of the earth. If he occupies any domain at all, it is that of the mind. His being depends on the human mind's ability to contemplate abstractly, which, as it happens, is exactly how the ego is generated as well.

Monotheism is the extension of an actualized ego, a reflection of the ego's gaze into the existential, cosmic mirror. Or perhaps the ego is the projection of God's image or self-idea into the world. Yahweh's singular nature reflects the singular nature of the ego. Like him, the ego is a unified isolate. And out of its own felt unity, the ego perceives the unity of the Self. This divine ratio is expressed to Moshe by Yahweh at Mount Horeb: *Ehyeh Asher Ehyeh* or "I am that I am" or "I will be there howsoever I will be there."[3]

The name *Yahweh* is an archaic form of the verb "to be." Yahweh tells Moshe, "I am he who is."[4] In other words, *I* am consciousness itself. If the Israelites ask for God's name, Yahweh tells Moshe to say to them, "I Am has sent me to you."[5] Moshe's experience is the moment the ego (as Moshe) peers into the abyss and, in mystical epiphany, becomes aware of its cosmic source: the Self (Yahweh). The Self is only cognized as a unity by a unified ego. In this way, the individual and God arise simultaneously. The terror and awe of this realization forces Moshe to turn his face away, unable to look directly upon the face of God.

The meaning of *Yahweh* corresponds to the cryptic letter *E* inscribed above the entrance of Apollo's temple at Delphi toward the middle of the first millennium BC, over five-hundred years after Moshe's experience at Mount Horeb. *E* is the present tense, second-person singular version of the verb *to be*, which means "You are" or "Thou art." Etched below *E* was the famous inscription *Gnothi sauton*, which means "Know thyself." Renee Descartes's most famous deduction, "I think, therefore I am," was surely inspired by the same epiphany that struck both Moshe and the person—rumored to be Pythagoras himself—who carved *E* into Apollo's temple. You are. I am. The presence of *I* and God emerge together.

The *I* is an awareness of the harmonious collision of uncountable quanta inside the present moment, "the moment where God is always to be found."[6] And if the present moment is where God is to be found, then this is where *I* has to be found as well, for there cannot be *I* without *Thou* in the same way that there cannot be black without white, love without hate, life without death. God locates itself in the present moment by casting an ego—each one calls itself *I*—which in turn projects God, or at least a God-image. The individual is a consequence of God's awareness of time as linear, a constriction of its omniscience to the diameter of an ego. God needs man in order to know; man needs God in order to know—you need I to manifest, just as I need you. "O Mohammed," God said, "hadst thou not been, I would not have created the sky."[7]

Literacy is the foundation upon which the ego and monotheism arise. The second commandment formulated at Mount Sinai, a seemingly bizarre one—*Thou shalt not make unto thee any graven image*—ties into the conflict between word (abstract) versus image (concrete). The book of Saint John opens with "In the beginning was the Word." "Word" comes from the Indo-european *wyrd,* which means to spin or turn, linking it to the whirling spirit of Yahweh, the *Logos,* and rational principle. Words are the supreme abstractions of the human mind, and more specifically, constructs of the left brain. Images are the responsibility of the right brain. To image or idolize Yahweh would be to constrict His totality to one of its many facets, an erroneous reduction and therefore blasphemous. Jews are the People of the Book: their religion is uniquely void of art or images of any kind.

Islam inherited a similar apprehension of images, as its devotees are expressly forbidden to image Allah or his prophet Muhammad. The famous arabesques of the early Islamic Period—in which it was strictly forbidden to depict human beings—are symptoms of this ban on images. Muhammad, though illiterate himself, discouraged depictions of objects and instead permitted only lines and colors.[8] This psychologically corresponds to the ego's inability to fathom the Self through the process of thought, because thinking is necessarily a categorization and thus an exercise in limiting. Like the *Word*, the Hebrew God is the supreme abstraction and therefore unthinkable, unimaginable, and unsayable, which is why uttering God's name is forbidden in Orthodox circles.

This helps us understand why Egypt's experiment with monotheism coincided with the resurrection of an alternative Egyptian writing style called *hieratic*, which was a phonetic, abstract form of writing that almost completely usurped the image-based hieroglyphic style of the Old Kingdom. The switch to *hieratic* parallels the Hyksos reign in Egypt, making it plausible that these Semitic kings helped re-popularize this writing form, given its stylistic similarity to the late Akkadian cuneiform long established in their homeland of Canaan.[9]

Unlike the richly imaged and colorful gods of the Old Kingdom (figures such as the crocodilian Sobek or the jackal-faced Set), the New Kingdom gods (such as Amon and Aton) who rose to prominence during the takeover of *hieratic*, were essentially imageless. Amon was the god of air who took on an invisible incarnation, and Aton was the sun god, depicted as a circular disk in the sky casting down beams of light into the mortal world below. About six centuries later, after the introduction of the alphabet into their societies, Greek philosophers would set aside the Greek pantheon in favor of the idea of a One or an Unlimited (*Aperion*) and, in one of their most literate and politically vibrant cities, invent democracy. The historical simultaneity of monotheism, abstract literacy, the individual and the ego, is not happenstance.

It is no coincidence that the birth of the individual originated with the Hebrews, whose culture was the first to require common literacy. Personal ancestry and personal names are uniquely common to the Bible. You will not find any other contemporary religious text so devoted to mortal individuals along with their names, lineages, legacies, fortunes, misfortunes, and personalities. We find the earliest examples of recognizably unique, developed individuals in the Old Testament, in contrast to any other contemporary epic of the Western world, such as the *Iliad*. Prominent figures of the Old Testament—like Avraham, Yitzhak, Yaakov, Yosef, Moshe, and David[i]—are certainly archetypal heroes, but personal in that we find in their stories, especially with the later figures like David, relatable individuals and destinies not prescribed by fate (unlike Achilles or Oedipus). Nor are these figures batted around by whimsical gods and goddesses, but rather are animated by a presence of self and a free will rooted in the psychological and moral development of their tribal god. The formulation of the proto-individual initiated during the Neolithic and Bronze ages was elaborated spectacularly in the minds of Avraham and his descendants over the course of centuries. The Voice promised Avraham, "I will make a great nation of you and will give you blessing and will make your name great."[10]

Cahill points out that many of the social themes of the modern age ultimately come out of this worldview. When you consider the psychological contributions of the Jews to Western thought, it is difficult to not imagine yourself as Jewish in a very real way. "We can hardly get up in the morning or cross the street without being Jewish," Cahill says. "We dream Jewish dreams and hope Jewish hopes. Most of our best words, in fact—*new, adventure, surprise, unique, individual, person, vocation, time, history, future, progress, spirit, faith, hope, justice*—are the gifts of the Jews."[11]

These words make little sense without the point of view of the individual. The *new* only happens to an individual who

---

[i] For the Old Testament patriarchs traditionally spelled in English as Abraham, Isaac, Jacob and Joseph, and Moses, I use an English spelling closer to the original sound of Hebrew supplied by Hebrew scholar and translator Everett Fox. I maintain the traditional English spelling of *Abraham* when I use the name in an adjectival manner, as in "Abrahamic religions."

breaks from the circle of time, like an *entrepreneur*, which means to begin something, to undertake. A *vocation* is a personal, or individual, calling. *History* is conceivable only from a specific reference point in the present. We *hope* for something better only as individuals who believe in a real future. The myth of *progress*, so dear to us, began with the Jews.

It is all too easy for us modern readers to dismiss ancient, literary products like the Old Testament as backward thinking and then congratulate ourselves on our own assumed moral and social progress. But if we read the pages of the Old Testament closely enough, we will find the seeds of liberalism and humanism, germs that took root in Western thinking three-thousand years ago and sprouted some two-and-a-half millennia later during the Renaissance and Enlightenment periods. Deuteronomy echoes many of the modern values we cherish today:

> "Judge with equity between each man and his brother or a sojourner. You are not to (specially) recognize a face in judgement; as the small, so the great, you are to hear them out."[12]

> "Each person, no matter their status, was to be heard. So you are to love the sojourner, for sojourners you were in the land of Egypt."[13]

Strangers were to be protected and honored. What is astounding about this admonition is that it was written during a period when only elites, gods, and monarchs were relevant enough to make it into what precious little media there was. In no other text of antiquity do we witness the extension of attention and compassion toward society's disenfranchised, or at least not to the extent that it was codified.

> "At the end of three years, you are to bring out all the tithing of your produce, in that year, and you are to deposit (it) within your gates. And when he comes, the Levite and the sojourner, the orphan and the widow that are within your gates, they will eat and be satisfied."[14]

The Hebrews knew what it was like to be the lowest of the low, for Yahweh reminds them: "You must bear in mind that a serf were you in the land of Egypt, and Yahweh your God redeemed you."[15]

We can nearly hear Christ's moniker of "whatsoever you do to the least of your brothers and sisters, you do unto me" echoing below the text.

The Hebrews' insistence on the essentiality of the individual shaped the foundation of Western thought. It informed the thinking of medievalist Roger Bacon, who proposed that experiment should be the principal factor in verifying scientific inquiry.[ii] It informed the thinking of eighteenth-century Voltaire, who advocated for individual freedom of thought in the face of a censoring Catholic Church. It inspired the wisdom of philosopher William James, who regarded the individual mind as the quintessential instrument capable of ascertaining truth from objective reality. It is also the heart of Thomas Jefferson's Declaration of Independence, which describes the "self-evident" truth that all men are created equal. Values of the individual began to appear in the second millennium BC with the Hebrews, filtered down through the ages, and flowed into the zeitgeist of the modern era. The individual was born with the Jews.

[ii] Despite its desire to eliminate or at least minimize the infiltration of subjective experience into its findings, scientific inquiry is in fact dependent on subjective experience because an experiment requires a subject to conduct it onto an object in the first place. Reality cannot be experienced without a subject. The words *experiment* and *experience* share the same Latin root.

CHAPTER 12:

Job: The Archetype of Personal Tragedy

This I know: that my Avenger lives, and he, the last of all, will take his stand upon this Earth, and in my flesh shall I see God.

~ Job[1]

The next milestone for consciousness is reflected in the Book of Job. It is a story about a righteous man whose life is destroyed by a bet between God and Satan. Satan approaches Yahweh and insists that Job is not as righteous as he appears. He wagers that Job would curse Yahweh if ever he were to lose his fortune. God agrees to test Job and has Satan utterly wreck his life. Satan robs Job of his wealth and livestock, kills his servants and children, and riddles Job with diseases. In the end, Job morally survives the experience, and despite the intense suffering he endures, he does *not* curse Yahweh and turn bitter toward the world, as Satan had predicted. Popularly, the story of Job confronts the question of why bad things happen to good people. "The Lord gave, and the Lord hath taken away."[2]

But there is something else going on in this story: the transformation of consciousness. In the Book of Job, for the first time in the Old Testament, Yahweh engages a person independent of their relationship to Israel. Whereas Yahweh dealt with Avraham, Yitzhak, Yaakov, Yosef, and Moshe as

Israelites in the context of the nation's fate,[3] in the case of Job, God approaches him as an individual.[4] Through this direct encounter, God sees himself through the eyes of Job's ego. In other words, God *self-reflects* through Job and is transformed as a result. "Whoever knows God has an effect on him."[5]

What does consciousness see when it looks upon itself for the first time? It sees an unconscious, primitive being. Yahweh's behavior throughout the Torah oscillates between extremes: tyrannical and just, loving and cruel, vengeful and merciful. His unpredictable nature reminds us of a child or an animal, "At one moment Yahweh behaves as irrationally as a cataclysm; the next moment he wants to be loved, honored, worshipped, and praised as just."[6] He often breaks his own moral rules in outbursts of anger.

This clues us in on something close to an answer to one of the more obvious yet generally unasked questions of the story of Job: why does Yahweh turn so readily against his faithful servant? Why, if Job was "a sound and honest man who fears God and shuns evil,"[7] does Yahweh test him with almost no hesitation whatsoever? The poet who wrote the Book of Job seems to leave the question hanging. Even after Job's livestock, servants, and children are murdered and Job remains steady having "committed no sin," and does not "reproach God,"[8] Yahweh encourages Satan to go further. "He (Job) persists in his integrity still," says Yahweh to Satan. "You achieved nothing by provoking me to ruin him." But Satan, acting as Yahweh's own shadow, his "doubting thought,"[9] replies that besides robbing him of his wealth and children, Yahweh needs only to ruin Job's health, and *then* Job "will curse you to your face."[10]

"Very well," says Yahweh, "but spare his life." Job is then smitten with horrific diseases. To put this into perspective, Job's situation is like having your house repossessed by the tax authorities, your life savings lost, your children die on their way to school, and your doctor hand you a terminal cancer diagnosis all in one week. When put in such terms and truly understood, the Book of Job brings your mind to the case limit of personal tragedy, which is what makes Job's story archetypal. Job is the archetype of personal tragedy. He is the one who has done everything right, amassed wealth, produced a family, and created happiness—then has it all taken away. Job is the good father whose daughter dies in a drunk-driving accident…he is the child of famine with an oversized head and a swollen belly, scrounging for food scraps…the mother standing numb before her son's casket…the infant dying of syphilis. The Book of Job speaks the harsh truth of a fate possibly worse than death meted out to a good or innocent person.

Job, ravaged by ulcers and sores and all but destroyed, insists on justice, remaining true to himself and firm in the face of Yahweh's undeserved wrath:

> "For he is not human like me: impossible for me to answer him or appear alongside him in court. There is no arbiter between us to lay his hand on both, to stay his rod from me, or keep away his daunting terrors. Nonetheless, unafraid of him, I shall speak, since I do not see myself like that at all. Since I have lost all taste for life, I shall give free rein to my complaining. I shall let my embittered soul speak out. I shall say to God, 'Do not condemn me; tell me what your case is against me.'"[11]

Job knows he is innocent. "The only thing he can be blamed for," Jung points out, "is his incurable optimism in believing that he can appeal to divine justice. In this he is mistaken, as Yahweh's subsequent words prove."[12] Yahweh's subsequent words are something along the lines of, "Who are *you*, useless worm of a mortal, to question *me*, the Creator, and appeal to fairness or the contracts I made with Avraham and Noah? Show me your godlike power." To quote Yahweh's response verbatim: "Where were you when I laid the Earth's foundations? Tell me, since you are so well-informed!"

Yahweh continues this tirade for a while, reminding Job of his divine feats and power without giving Job a rational answer as to why he ruined him or any hint of a chance at divine justice. Jung points out that it is as if Yahweh were not really addressing Job, for it is certainly not the broken and battered Job who needs any more convincing that Yahweh is all-powerful. Herein Jung senses the hair-raising question of this story: who, then, is Yahweh *really* talking to?

> "Yahweh sees something in Job which we would not ascribe to him but to God, that is, an equal power which causes him to bring out his whole power apparatus and parade it before his opponent. Yahweh projects onto Job a sceptic's face which is hateful to him because it is his own, and which gazes at him with an uncanny and critical eye. He is afraid of it, for only in the face of something frightening does one let off a cannonade of references to one's power, cleverness, courage, invincibility, etc."[13]

Yahweh is addressing Himself, his own self-doubt, through Job. "Job is no more than the outward occasion for an inward process of dialectic in God."[14] God's inner dialectic ranges from questions about God's infinite wisdom...

> "Who decided [the Earth's] dimensions, do you know? Or who stretched the measuring line across it? Who supports its pillars at their bases? Who laid its cornerstone? Who pent up the sea behind closed doors? Have you an inkling of the extent of the Earth? Tell me all about it if you have! Will lightning flashes

> come at your command? Who endowed the ibis with wisdom and gave the cock his intelligence? Whose skill details every cloud?"[15]

...to monologues about God's proclivity for wrath and vengeance...

> "Has your arm the strength of God's? Can your voice thunder as loud? Come on, display your majesty and grandeur. Robe yourself in splendor and glory. Let the fury of your anger burst forth, humble the haughty at a glance! At a glance, bring down all the proud, strike down the wicked where they stand. Bury the lot of them in the ground. Shut them, every one, in the dungeon. And I shall be the first to pay you homage."[16]

...to his mastery of evil, the primeval power of Behemoth and Leviathan, symbols of God's untamable animal instinct and the screaming chaos swirling beneath the surface of the order of existence:

> "But look at Behemoth, my creature, just as you are! He is the first of the works of God. Under the lotus he lies; he hides among the reeds in the swamps. Who is going to catch him by the eyes or put poles through his nose? Leviathan too! Can you catch him with a fishhook or hold his tongue down with a rope? He has no equal on Earth, being created without fear. He looks the haughtiest in the eye: of all the lordly beasts, he is king."[17]

God's inner dialectic is a process of self-revelation. *Who does all of this but me? Who is responsible for Leviathan and Behemoth but me?* "I form the light, and create darkness. I make peace, and create evil. I, the Lord, do all these things."[18]

This divine self-revelation occurs because Job stands up and demands that Yahweh explain himself.

> "Job, by his insistence on bringing his case before God, even without hope of a hearing, had stood his ground and thus created the very obstacle that forced God to reveal his true nature...Here, Yahweh comes up against a man who stands firm, who clings to his rights until [God] is compelled to give way to brute force. [Job] has seen God's face and the unconscious split in his nature. God was now known."[19]

Job thus witnesses firsthand the "inner antimony" of God.[20] That is to say, Job sees the coexistence of evil and good in God, and in so doing experiences for himself the union of opposites; a *coincidentia oppositorum*.

The heard and the seen merge. Job experiences the numinous and finds himself in the presence of what Rudolph Otto called the "wholly other."[21] Job is at one with *That* (hence at-one-ment), and finally understands the purpose of his ruination: to be the sacrificial vessel through which God becomes self-conscious. This, as Rivkah Scharf Kluger notes, "gives meaning to [Job's] suffering and liberation of his soul."[22] At first Job is concerned with his innocence and clings to it like we do when, after tragedy visits us, we look up at the Void with resentment and shout, "Why me? What have I done to deserve this?" We ask these questions from the perspective of an ego that will not, as Edward Edinger declares, "grant the existence of a greater reality than one's personal desires. Job asked why his misery should happen to him. The answer that emerges...is so that he may see God."[23] Job experiences Totality. "Before, I knew you only by hearsay, but now, having seen you with my own eyes, I retract what I have said, and repent in dust and ashes."[24]

At the end of the story, Yahweh restores Job's fortunes, blessing him with double the wealth he had before and granting him another seven sons and three daughters. But the cosmic consequence of Job's experience is the moral elevation of man above God, which precipitates God's incarnation in the form of a human being. It is analogous to the plight of a torturer who cannot shake the feeling that his victim, whom he brought so low, somehow has come out on top. In spite of the immense show of power, in spite of his victim's pleadings and admissions of inferiority, the torturer walks away behind, the victim ahead. Yahweh's domination rings hollow in the face of a morally superior victim whose eyes peer back at him from a broken body and seem to say, "Your actions come from a place of ignorance. I see why you do this." In the end, Job "stands morally higher than Yahweh...the creature has surpassed the creator,"[25] and now that Job has seen him, Yahweh's self-reflection is not an option: it is forced through Job's witnessing.

"Self-reflection becomes an imperative necessity, and for this Wisdom is needed." Wisdom is Sophia, Yahweh's playmate from the beginning of time, "beside the master craftsman, delighting him day after day, ever at play in his presence, at play everywhere on Earth, delighting to be with the children of men."[26] Sophia has been remembered at the precise cosmic moment in which God gains knowledge of himself through own creature's eyes. This accounts for why the Book of Job exists within the literary category of the biblical "Wisdom Books," alongside Proverbs, Psalms, Ecclesiastes, etc. Wisdom reappears at this historical moment, and the literature admitted into the Old Testament reflects that. Yahweh is reminded that he must become a human. "He, the guardian of justice, knows that every wrong must be expiated, and Wisdom knows that moral law is above even him.

Because his creature has surpassed him, he must regenerate himself."[27]

The torturer must now trade places with the victim. God will, as Job did, be the sacrificial lamb. He must fully abandon himself into the vessel of man through the Christ-figure who, this time, unlike the unconscious Adam, will be an ego conscious of its relationship to the Self. Yahweh must be born a "Son of Man," suffer like Job, and take it one step further: he must make the ultimate sacrifice—dying as an incarnated ego. This great act, the Incarnation, becomes the epicenter of Christianity because it redeems both God and human life.

Yahweh, having seen and reckoned with his own dark side through Job, opens up. His possessiveness and jealousy gradually subside, and "the 'children of Israel' take something of a second place in comparison to the 'children of men.'" The Incarnation of Christ signals the beginning of a New Covenant (hence: New Testament) with a transformed God. Through his encounter with Job, Yahweh begins his transformation into the gentle and loving Father of the New Testament. The God-to-man exchange in Job alters the nature of God and the nature of man.

CHAPTER 13:

When the West Learned How to Think

Philosophy is a historical phenomenon...it is a mistake to think that just because history took this turn, good philosophy has to be something that ultimately is irrelevant to our life, to the life of those we live with and our life with them, and to the life of our communities and societies. And it certainly would be a mistake to project our conception of philosophy, as a rather academic enterprise of developing philosophical theories, back on the ancients.

~ Michael Frede[1]

At the same time the Book of Job was written (roughly the sixth century BC), some eight-hundred miles away on the western edge of Asia, a new class of thinker surfaced in the Greek world: the philosopher. *Philosophy* comes from the words *philo* (love) and *sophos* (wisdom), meaning *love of wisdom*. These lovers of *sophos* appear at the same historical moment in which Sophia reemerges into Old Testament literature. This is eerie when you consider the fact that the Hebrews and Greeks would not have had any knowledge of each other for at least another two-hundred years.

The first philosophers were the Presocratics (those who preceded Socrates and his intellectual descendants, Plato and Aristotle). They carried magi-like auras, quite different from the dryness we associate with philosophers today. The Presocratics wanted to discover the stuff of the world (*kosmos*). The world, they thought, could no longer be explained by the tired stories of fickle Olympians mingling with mortals. The world made sense, somehow. Their search is summed up in a question posed near the turn of the sixth century BC by the very first philosopher, Thales of Miletus: *what is the single element of which the world is made?*

The Presocratics argued endlessly about this question for the next two centuries. Thales himself proposed that water must be the primary element in everything. Anaximenes said it was air. Empedocles would later say that it was a mixture of water, air, earth, and fire. Anaximander thought it could not be material but must be abstract, something he called *aperion* (the unlimited). Heraclitus declared there was no substance at all underlying reality, just change mediated by the *Logos* (rational principle). To Parmenides, on the other hand, the primary element was an unchanging constant he called *sein*. For Pythagoras, it was number; for Anaxagoras, it was mind; for the Atomists Leucippius and Democritus, it was all nothing but atoms (*atoma* means *unsplittable)* and the Void. They believed that matter did not emerge from mind, but that mind emerged from matter. It is no wonder that Democritus is often referred to as the great-grandfather of modern science.

By the time Plato and Aristotle appeared around the end of the fifth century BC, the foundation of Being had been established by the Presocratics. Plato formed his metaphysics from Socrates, Parmenides, Anaxagoras, and Pythagoras. According to Plato, Being was an eternal, unchanging intellect whose various conceptions were contained in a world of forms. An abstract hyperspace, the world of forms held the one, the good, the true, the beautiful, and the just. Taking the lead from Pythagoras, Plato also believed that the forms were eternal, mathematical formulae, abstract constructs of the chief intellect projected into the receptacle (*hupodoche*) of three-dimensional space. The *hupodoche* receives and transposes these projections into the geometrical figures of the visible world. Everything, according to Plato, is made up of basic triangles.

Like every notable student, Aristotle contradicted his teacher. Whereas Plato was an idealist—someone who thinks ideas are more real than the material world—Aristotle was a materialist, someone who thinks the material world is more real than ideas. Ultimate reality is immanent, *here,* not transcendent and over *there.* Plato's forms, according to Aristotle, are not floating around architecting material reality from the vantage of perfect hyperspace, but instead reside within the objects themselves. There is no disembodied form of desk-ness suspended in a perfect world of ideas. The form of the desk was conceived in the mind of the carpenter who built the desk. The material of the desk is primary, its form secondary.

Aristotle would have felt more comfortable at dinner with Democritus and Leucippius than with Pythagoras and Parmenides. But Aristotle was not a proto-nu-atheist who believed only in matter and the Void. He perceived the immortality of the soul and accepted the Parmenidean notion of a motionless Being, which he termed the "Unmoved Mover." And like Anaxagoras, Aristotle thought of this mover as a cosmic intellect responsible for the movement of the cosmos. It was both the ultimate source of all individual substances (*ousiai*) and the attractor toward which they strove in pursuit of their own perfect state; it was both the beginning and the end of all things. Aristotle believed that the Unmoved Mover was also the root of the human intellect and the source of human enlightenment. Despite a certain overlap in his thinking with the Friends of the Forms, Aristotle was entrenched in the camp of the Sons of Earth. The Sons of Earth were materialists who counted the Empodicleans, Atomists, Stoics, and Epicureans in their ranks.

Aristotle's dissent from his master Plato split Greek thought, and hence Western thought, forevermore into two strands: Platonism and Aristotelianism. Platonism is idealism, Aristotelianism is materialism. Each would fall in and out of fashion over the course of the next two millennia. But all subsequent Western thinkers, from Plotinus and Saint Augustine of Hippo to Saint Thomas Aquinas and Roger Bacon to Renee Descartes and Isaac Newton to Friedreich Nietzsche to Albert Einstein and Werner Heisenberg, built their ideas and models of reality from one of these two vantage points.

Whatever the philosophers thought reality was made of, the concerning question is *why* did they suddenly care? In Hesiod's treatment of Greek myth, existence sprang from Chaos, the equivalent of the Babylonian goddess, Tiamat, whose body was *the world*. This seemed to be good enough for everyone in ancient Greece. But then this changed with the philosophers. They began to make *the world* a subject of analysis, something their ancient predecessors had never bothered to do. They had not bothered because attempting to understand and dissect something as immanent as the very world itself was an inconceivable intellectual exercise. The fact that Thales' question—*what is the basic element of the world?*—could even be asked, tells us that a novel form of consciousness had infiltrated Greece.

CHAPTER 14:

How the Alphabet Changed Our Minds

It is only as language becomes written down that it becomes possible to think about it...in the alphabetized document, the medium became objectified. There it was, reproduced perfectly in the alphabet, not a partial image but the whole of it, no longer just a function of 'me' the speaker but a document with an independent existence.

~ *Eric Havelock*[1]

Before the philosophers, the ancient Greek mind was preconscious. It interfaced with the world through a polytheistic mythos. Unlike Old Testament characters such as Avraham, Moshe, Yosef, and David, Greek deities like Zeus, Hera, Aphrodite, and Athena were not evolving individuals with unique, human outlooks. They were gods beyond time and the world, always occupied by the same concerns, doing the same things over and over, never changing. This is because they are merely components of a total personality. They represent archetypal *facets* of the Self—the king, the bride, the lover, the warrior, etc. Edward Edinger comments on this:

> "Psychologically, we can consider the idea of an Olympian realm as a projection onto the outer world... of an inner state. It would be a state that is eternal,

> unchanging, and a realm of the spirit, as opposed to matter...We are left with the conclusion that there exists an eternal psyche, or something symbolized by an eternal psyche, that is of greater duration than the ego...In [Jung's] purely psychological view, the heavenly realm of the Greek gods is seen as a part of the human psyche which is beyond time and space and beyond the control of the conscious personality. The early images such as that of the Olympians are understood as translations of psychological realities into external ones."[2]

In other words, the Olympian realm reflected a portion of the psyche beyond the control of an ego—that is to say, an *unconscious* portion of the psyche. The Olympian realm mirrored the existence of an unstructured psyche, a Greek proto-ego. But this would begin to change around the seventh century BC. To be sure, the gods continued to be important to the Greeks. To some degree, people worshiped and dedicated sacrifices to the figures of Olympus for at least another millennium, but the heyday of the gods was over. They would gradually fade into the cultural periphery, thanks to the effects of a new form of consciousness imported into Greece by way of a Trojan horse called "the alphabet."

Linear B, the variation of cuneiform used by the Mycenaeans and much of the ancient world during the second millennium BC, virtually disappeared in the twelfth century BC. It would not be until sometime late in the ninth or early eighth century BC that literacy reappeared and brought historical light back into Greece. But this time, instead of Linear B, the alphabet—a simpler and more abstract form of literacy—took over.

The alphabet is the youngest of the ancient forms of writing. It was invented sometime during the second millennium BC by one or multiple cultures in the Levant—probably through some unorganized effort of the Phoenicians, Canaanites, and Hebrews—although some credit Egypt as the originator.[i]

All written languages have a code of characters. In an alphabet, those characters are called "letters." Each letter stands for a sound of speech, called a "phoneme." Combine a few of these phonemes to form a word or a name. You can do this endlessly to generate different words. You cannot do this as easily with a system like cuneiform because its symbols represent entire syllables (rather than a single particle of sound like a letter) which renders a single cuneiform symbol useful for a specific word or two but then often sidelined otherwise. This means that with cuneiform you must have hundreds of symbols to express a single language. Alphabets typically contain thirty or fewer phonemes (letters), which makes them simpler and easier to master than the other two options in the ancient world—cuneiform and hieroglyphics—which comprised six-hundred and seven-hundred symbols, respectively.[3] Five-year-olds can, and do, learn the entire alphabet, but would have no such luck with cuneiform and hieroglyphics.

Another power of alphabetic letters is that they can be adapted by any language system to create that language's unique set of sounds. This adaptability has made alphabets viral. As of the beginning of the twenty-first century, over three-quarters of the world's population live in countries where an alphabet-based script forms the basis of the national writing system.[4] Compared to the logographic or image-based literacy of the Far East (Chinese, for instance), alphabetic languages are syllabic, in that their signs represent sounds rather than images; linear, in that their letters are structured sequentially; and abstract, in that the shapes of their words have no connection to the thing they signify. For example, the shapes of the letters in the word *mountain* do not together visually resemble a mountain.

[i] Those interested in the history of the alphabet should read *Letter Perfect: The Marvelous History of Our Alphabet from A to Z*, by David Sacks (New York: Broadway Books, 2003).

The alphabet objectifies reality. Words hold the external world and the "things" in it in a psychological stasis of signification. This effect was especially powerful for the psyche of the Greeks because their alphabet was different in one important way from the original, imported, Semitic model. The Semitic alphabet contained only consonants, not vowels. This meant that when reading Hebrew, a speaker had to *infer* the vowels to speak the word, which was only possible if they learned the language by hearing it spoken aloud. Thus, to read Hebrew, you needed to know how to speak it. This gave Hebrew an embedded subjectivity.

This is not so with Greek, because the Greeks added vowels to the alphabet. This made Greek an entirely objective literary system—one which the Romans copied and conveyed to Western Europe and, by extension, to you, since you are reading these words. Adding vowels to the alphabet removes subjective interaction with the world. Since language is how we consciously interface with reality, the addition of vowels also demystifies our connection with the world and makes it feel separate from us. The alphabet lifted the Greek mind into a separated, conscious relationship with the world.

And so roughly one century after the alphabet's arrival in the Greek world, we see the first emergent signs of Greek philosophical thinking, a pattern of consciousness correspondent to how an ego-conscious, analytical left brain separates itself from reality. We can see this by the two things the Presocratics more or less agreed on: (1) there is an eternal, unchanging Being behind reality,[ii] and (2) the visible world derives from that Being and is thus trivial and illusory. These commonalities point to the fundamental psychological change that happened in Greece.

[ii] Heraclitus is the exception because he did not believe in an unchanging ultimate. Even so, his concept of the *Logos*, the rational principle that orders reality into existence, seems evidence of his own intellectual contact with the Self.

The first point corresponds to the emergence of ego from the Self. As the Greek psyche condensed and became conscious, it, like the Hebrews, became aware of a unified Other. Whether they called it water, the unlimited (*aperion*), *Logos*, intellect, mind (*nous*), *sein*, or the One, the philosophers tried to encapsulate this homogenous thing or substance or Being into a concise word or idea. Without the psychological reprogramming of the alphabet, the Greek ego could not have gained a separated vantage point from which to objectively examine reality and become aware of its unified source, the Self.

The second principle—that the visible world deriving from the One is illusory—emerges from the ego's perspective. The alphabet's system supplies the subject-object modality (me versus not-me), tenses (past, present, and future) and parts of speech (nouns) that the left brain uses to cut the world into separate things (trees, cars, glass, tables, sky, clouds) and flatten eternity into a line. That there seemed to be something eternal behind or beyond the visible world and responsible for its makeup, clues us that ego-consciousness had come online and sensed the fleeting nature of its time-bound illusions. This Greek metaphysic would become fundamental to Christianity. In Paul's second letter to the Corinthians 4:18, he writes from a Jewish mind that is thoroughly Hellenistic: "What we aim for is not visible but invisible. Visible things are transitory, but invisible things are eternal."

Xenophanes, another Presocratic of the sixth century BC, felt the secondary nature of the ego-world. He distinguished between two types of cognition: *oida* (knowledge) and *doxa* (opinion). Probably frustrated by his own ability to attain conscious understanding of the ultimate, Xenophanes was pessimistic about the human capacity to access what lay behind the curtain.

Xenophanes realized the conundrum of it all. Ultimate reality is infinite, acategorical, and indefinite. It is not sayable (*doxa*) because encapsulating it in a word squeezes it through a thought process that finites, categorizes, and defines it. When this is done, attainment becomes impossible. The parallel between the Hebrew taboo of uttering Yahweh's name and the nonsayableness of the Greek *aperion* is unmistakable here. This is what Xenophanes meant when he famously declared "Certain truth has no man seen, nor will there ever be a man who knows about the gods and about everything of which I speak; for even if he should fully succeed in saying what is true, even so he himself does not know it, but over all things there is wrought opinion."[5] The matter is summarized well by Lao Tzu, a Chinese contemporary of Xenophanes: "He who knows, does not speak. He who speaks, does not know."

To the philosophers, the world could be explained, and it was up to the human intellect to explain it. We have inherited their obsession. Their compulsion with finding an ultimate scheme of reality parallels our own fixity of purpose of doing so today. Modern physicists have been hard at work for the last century to attain a unified field theory, a cooperation between Einstein's theory of gravity, which explains the workings of the universe on massive scales, and quantum field theory, which explains the workings of reality on sub-atomic scales. Since we still have not satisfactorily answered Thales of Miletus's question, *what is the essential nature of reality?*, we may look back with humility at the efforts of the philosophers whose best guesses seem to be about as good as our own.

The critical difference between the philosophers and their ancient predecessors was the ability to think in the abstract, a byproduct of left-brain thinking exacerbated by the alphabet. That the world could be made of something *not in the world*, like the *unlimited* or a cosmic *mind*, had never occurred to anyone in the Greek world before this. Anaximander was the first to reject that the world was made of something fundamentally concrete.

The gravity of this kind of thinking is largely unnoticed by most.

All ancient cultures fought bloody wars over things like gold, women, land, and natural resources—notice all of these things are tangible things *in* the world—but never once did any of them bother to fight wars over *ideas,* like what gods their enemies worshipped or what political or economic system they subscribed to. Fighting over abstractions, rather than stuff, is only about four-thousand years old, and it began when the Hebrews invaded Canaan sometime during the twelfth century BC. The Hebrews were the first culture *ever* to invade another over an abstraction, an idea. Never before the alphabet had the abstract seemed more real than the material to the human mind. This kind of thinking is what led many presocratic philosophers to the conclusion that the world was, at its most fundamental level, abstract. This would forever change how the West thought. The ability to think from the abstract allowed us to objectify the contents of the world and sometimes confuse the abstract for what is real.

Contemporary with Greece's first abstract thinker was Herodotus, the West's first historian. No surprise, since the alphabet reinforces the cognitive preferences of the side of the brain that experiences time sequentially. The ancient Greeks had never bothered before this moment to document the actions of their past in a linear flow of cause and effect. Before Herodotus, the closest thing the Greeks had to a historian was Homer. But his cyclical stories were more like songs, blurring lines between eternity and time, fiction and fact, and gods and mortals. Herodotus, on the other hand, was only concerned with time, facts, and mortality. He tried to rationally apprehend the world by laying out a serial flow of events leading up to the present. He established the Western habit of explaining the present by examining its past. Of course, the Greeks held onto their notion of fate. The future was to ultimately repeat the past for them, but with the effects of alphabetic thinking at work, they objectified eternity, took apart its contents, and laid them out one event after another.

Swept up in alphabetic consciousness, Anaximander was also the first Greek to write in prose. Before Anaximander's time, everyone wrote in *verse* style. Homer's *Iliad* and *Odyssey* were written in verse. Prose is linear. Sometimes prose was written in a spiral or right-to-left or left-to-right or up-down or as the ox plows a field, but always sequentially. Prose is the format of communication we use to get a task done (broken down into a series of steps). Poems are not effective or usually desired in this realm. Verse is musical by nature, using meter, rhythm, and metaphor—all of which are right-brain specialties—to convey meaning. In right-brained, egalitarian fashion, verse-style epics like the *Iliad* incorporate collective input from the culture over generations and are meant to be recited to an audience. Prose, on the other hand, is often both created and consumed by an individual. In this sense, epics are fashioned collectively and unconsciously, whereas prose is created individually and consciously.

Like prose, logic is also associated with the linearizing effects of the alphabet. Although logic as a formal intellectual practice made its earliest appearance with Parmenides, it was ultimately perfected by Aristotle, who came up with the *if-then* syllogistic structure we are familiar with today. Syllogistic thinking underpins rhetoric, business, military strategy, and science. Science uses a bottom-up form of logic called induction. It allows scientists to discover higher patterns in nature by observing the workings of minutiae on the ground—if I do *X* fifty times the same way and *Y* occurs every time, I can conclude that law *Z* exists. Thanks to Saint Thomas Aquinas's review of Aristotelian texts in the thirteenth century AD, Aristotelian logic became the ground of early modern science. In fact, modern science traces its origins to the moment Aquinas used

Aristotelian thinking to analyze the transubstantiation of the bread into the flesh of Christ in the Catholic sacrament of the Eucharist.

Given enough time under pressure from the alphabet, a culture will also begin to develop an abstract *identity*—an ego—both at the collective and individual level. This is why democracy was invented in Greece during the sixth century BC. A democracy is necessarily comprised of *individuals* whose collective will determines the direction of their state.

A Greek proto-nationalism appeared alongside democracy. There were roughly one-thousand city-states in classical Greece who identified themselves as distinct from their contemporaries, yet simultaneously part of a collective Greek consciousness rooted in the shared soil of religion, politics, and languages called Hellenism. During the fourth and third centuries BC, Hellenism infiltrated the Near East behind the armies of Alexander the Great.

The *I* took critical steps forward within the incubator of the Greek classical world. Propelled by the effects of the alphabet, the *I* divided the world through the thinking categories of the philosophers (these would become the *-ologies* of Western science), saw the One's reflection in the cosmic mirror, attained logic through Parmenides and Aristotle and used it to apprehend the nature of the world, linearized time to achieve a sense of history through Herodotus and Thucydides, gained a new form of identity through the masses, and atomized societies into democracy.

CHAPTER 15:

Fusing Greek and Hebrew Thought

Time is a thing posterior to the world. Therefore it would be correctly said that the world was not created in time, but that time had its existence in consequence of the world. For it is the motion of the heavens that has displayed the nature of time.

~ *Philo Judaeus*

Because the worldviews of the Greeks and the Hebrews were influenced by the alphabet, they evolved strikingly similar interfaces with the world. The alphabet catalyzed individual consciousness in both cultures, pervading them with democratic sensibilities. Although neither civic nor institutionalized, the social fabric of the Hebrew community was proto-democratic.

If credit for democracy must go one way, it must go to the Greeks. But the award for the development of the individual goes to the Hebrews. While both societies discovered the existence of the One, the Greeks recognized it only in a philosophical sense. They lacked a personal relationship with it, unlike the Hebrews, whose tribal destiny was linked inexorably to Yahweh. Both cultures also had a strong sense of linear thinking and as a result their own sense of history.

But it is from the friction between the Hebrew and Greek outlooks that the Western *I* was born. The world to the Greeks was space, whereas to the Hebrews it was time. These fundamental assumptions have become ours, and bringing them together has become the mission of the Western mind over the last two-thousand years.

For the Greeks, the world was first and foremost space. Note that Anaximander's *aperion* and Parmenides' *sein* are both defined in terms of space; *aperion* is the unlimited, extending in all directions, and *sein* is a sphere extending in all directions—a forerunner to the modern theory of the curvature of space. For the Greeks, reality *contained* things. And the things in it had form and were made of content (matter). Look at any object around you. Maybe you see a cup. Ask yourself, "What is it?" You will almost certainly start your answer with Greek assumptions. You might say the cup is a vessel or container (*form*) made of plastic or glass or, for the scientific sticklers, atoms (*content*).

This is another way of saying that the Greeks objectified reality, which requires that one stand apart from it and view it from a disembodied (abstract) vantage point as the subject. By objectifying the world, the Greeks *saw* it foremost. Because they prioritized space, the Greeks deprecated time and impressed it into the service of space. Space was so important to the Greeks that time was conceived in its image.[1]

This is how time took on its geometric character in the West. We often say a *point* of time, time*line* and then draw a line to depict time. Throughout this book, we've often distinguished between *line*ar time and circular or cyclical time. Both opposing concepts are geometric. For the Greeks, and for us, the past rests *behind* us and the future lies *ahead* of us. Days, weeks, months, and years are conceived in reference to the *spatial* positions of solar, lunar, and celestial *bodies* (which, again, are form). Consider the fact that many pagan Indo-European festivals center around solstices and equinoxes, which are designated by the relational positions of spatial bodies.

If time is a function of space, it makes sense then in *Timaeus* when Plato says that time is the moving image of eternity that proceeds by number. In other words, time is foremost an *image*, and more precisely, a restless gestalt of successive images driven by an abstraction called number. The active property here is not the concrete, feminine image, but instead the abstract, masculine number. Eternity, though typically thought of as endless duration, is best conceived in a Greek way as a fixed, immovable, incorruptible, spatial dimension in which all the content of the universe occurs and coexists.[i] Eternity was a spatial idea to the Greeks. Its structure was synonymous with a static Now, not endless chronological sequence.

Eternity is the *archetype* of time. Like matter or any other part of the phenomenal world, time is merely a miming of that archetype. When we tell time, we do not measure time so much as we measure eternity. And as we have seen with words, numbers also measure the world. In the same way we use words to split up the world into parts, we use numerical values to *measure* eternity and chunk it up into pieces like eons, eras, epochs, millennia, centuries, years, days, minutes, and so on. And just as happens with words, the modern mind often mistakes the symbol for what is empirically real. What are 10:30 am or 11:52 pm or the year 1501 BC or 2022 AD but simply different measurements of the same Now?

Because eternity was the archetypal ideal for the Greeks, time was evil. Time corroded, decayed, corrupted, and destroyed. On the other hand, geometry, space, and form were incorruptible—untouchable by time and therefore held in the highest esteem. The Greeks expressed this fundamental value hierarchy through the aesthetic ideal of the *kouros*, the beautiful,

[i] Expressions in Catholic prayers of "world without end," "life everlasting," and "forever and ever" are Greek contributions of eternality to the Judeo-Christian tradition.

male youth whose naked, perfect *form* is brought forth out of a block of marble, symbolizing undifferentiated, "virgin" matter. He stands publicly nude, forever young, brimming with energy, endlessly on the cusp of manhood and exempt from time.

If the Greeks primarily *saw* the world and thus clung to the power of image because of their spatial bias toward reality, the Hebrews *heard* the world temporally. In spite of the iconoclastic effects of the alphabet on Greek culture, most apparent in some of the regimes of the medieval Greek East, the classical Greeks busied themselves erecting sculptures of all sorts of figures, both human and nonhuman alike.[ii] But this was not so for the Hebrews. Their religion is entirely void of all images and art. Instead, the Hebrews emphasized what was heard and thus emphasized time. "The sense which is plainly made for successive impressions is hearing," noted Thorleif Boman. "We *see* the spatial and *hear* the temporal."[2] Yahweh always manifested to the Hebrews as a voice. He was *heard*, but never seen.[iii]The Hebrews understood reality as a series of *events*, rather than *things* in motion inside of space. Dinner time, quality time, high time, end time, bed time, play time, leisure time—these expressions show time coincident with its content as event, rather than an abstraction used to measure a snapshot of the motion of bodies in space. While for the Greeks reality is the co-existence of things in space, and time the movement of these things in unison (the image of succession), reality for the Hebrews is a succession of events (linearity, the Word). For the Hebrews, reality *is* time.

To better understand the Hebrew notion of time, consider a song. Although a song is heard as a succession of sounds and silences (positive and negative intervals), and greater still a chain of verses, choruses, and bridges, it is ultimately a living whole,

---

[ii] The medieval Greek world experienced waves of iconoclasm.

[iii] It is noteworthy that alphabetic writing, possibly original to the Hebrews themselves, is a pure representation of sound.

each of its parts bound to its unity. Its beginning, middle, and end points are subordinate to its greater life, which exists outside of time. To say the song exists in the past after it is finished, or in the future before we hear it, is not meaningful. The song is a living whole that transcends time. Its parts are simultaneously independent yet contemporaneous with the total song.

In this same way, each individual Hebrew felt themselves to be part of a transpersonal national consciousness—that national entity, Israel, which in turn was married to a greater cosmic consciousness. Israel is the wife of Yahweh.[iv] H. Wheeler Robinson called this mode of being the *corporate personality*, a revolutionary innovation that we take for granted today. The Hebrews could psychologically range across past and future and become contemporaneous with either a member of their tribe or with the tribe as a whole. We are all familiar with this state of consciousness. This is a nation. The nation of Israel is best understood as a collective person that started with Avraham: "I will make a great nation of you and will give you blessing and will make your name great."[3] Note that "you" is used collectively here. This is psychological transcendence. The Hebrews discovered an inner life, a *personal* experience connected up to a greater consciousness.

Consider the idea of sacrifice in the story of Cain and Abel. Cain does not make the proper kind of sacrifices and becomes miserable for it, while Abel's sacrifices bring him fortune and win him admiration. This story is as much about shaping reality with the mind's discovery of time as it is about fratricide and jealousy.[4] Cain and Abel were participating in the project of doing (the right or wrong) things now for the sake of their future selves.

By making the right sacrifices in the present, I can ensure a particular kind of future because I acknowledge the existence

[iv] This was the covenant established by Moshe at Mount Sinai. The ten commandments are the obligations of the marriage pact between the Hebrews and Yahweh. "'It will not be like the covenant I made with their ancestors, when I took them by the hand to lead them out of Egypt, because they broke My covenant, though I was husband to them,' declares the Lord." Jeremiah 31:32

of a future me and become contemporaneous with that future me, while that future me looks back on my present self. *How will I feel tomorrow if I do what I'm about to do? If I do X now, I will have to give up Y tomorrow. What would I like my life to look like in five years?* This capability constitutes the core being of an ego-conscious individual.

My name is a word I use to maintain a continuous identity across time, a continuum of self-reflection. Eventually I die, but my descendants live on. If I've raised them to become conscious individuals, then they, too, psychologically range across the past and future within their own lifespan by tying their stream of *I* to a name and, greater still, to a lineage or family or tribe. The names change with each new generation, but this continuous *I* flows from lifespan to lifespan, overlapping with itself in linear time due to the co-existence of generations. This is a community. Upon becoming aware of its individual and collective identities simultaneously, the *I* naturally begins to *remember* and *record* itself, which is to say it becomes *historical*.[v]

Like an individual, a community also weighs out sacrificing certain things in the present for the sake of its future self, and in so doing becomes contemporaneous with itself across time and thereby conscious of its history. This is to achieve a *national* consciousness. This is why the Hebrews are considered the first people of history. Their approach to time was personal.

The Greeks shared gods, politics, language and ideas in their classical period, but they did not, by contrast, together constitute a nation.[vi] Although they had a scientific sense of history, they had little sense of the importance of personal history, so the

---

[v] This is probably tied to the taboo among Orthodox Jews of naming a child after the living.

[vi] They did possess a sense of collective consciousness tied to their city-state. Athens is like Israel in that it was made up of a collection of individuals called Athenians who were psychologically connected to something greater than themselves (Athens). In the same way that Israel is the wife of Yahweh, Athens is both female (the goddess *Athena* is the namesake of Athens) and existentially bound up with the supreme god, Zeus. Myth has it that Athena was born out of Zeus's forehead which is incidentally where *I* is located for many of us. In this way, her existence echoes the idea that ego-consciousness is a thought generated by the Self and that the abstraction of nationhood is a left-brain construct dependent on a collection of people who experience themselves ego-consciously.

Greeks were truly non-historical. The future was thus always to be a repeat of the past. Even Herodotus ultimately understood the past in the context of his culture's ideal of eternity—an ideal which existed beyond this world as *sein*, the unalterable, the unchanging. Subconsciously for him, the future *had* to be a repetition of the past.

But a non-historical worldview is an impossible state of consciousness for a *corporate personality*. The fact that the Hebrews felt themselves as a corporate person is arguably why they are also considered the people of revelation. For when God revealed himself to one of them, it meant revelation to all of them even if unconsciously. For the Israelites, reality was God's active and continuous revelation of himself through time.

In this same way, mystical experience—*satori, moksha, nirvana, the beatific vision*—as a reunion of Self and ego, means becoming contemporaneous with the whole of universal consciousness; it is to be psychologically identical with God. It is, quite literally, the universe experiencing itself at once. This produces the effect of waking up. To know God is to know your *true* self as the river of time. In this way, the purpose of ego-consciousness is to figure out what God really is by way of union with him. Out of these deep, mystical insights on being an individual, Judaism fathered the other two major religions of the West.

While the Greek philosopher thought of the world objectively, and therefore causally, logically, and scientifically, the Hebrew felt it religiously and personally. The past to the Greek was scientifically describable—events like the Peloponnesian War were documented serially—whereas the past for the Hebrew was psychological and historical in that the future was personal and held the possibility of being different from the past. Progress and change were possible. For the Greeks, the *aperion* existed somewhere beyond as the unchanged, not in the corrupt and fluctuating phenomenal world of nature, of which human history was a part (and thus unimportant, archetypal, and ultimately unreal). The opposite was true for the Hebrews. For them, history was personal. They were participating in the story of the ongoing revelation of God, the unfolding of a drama progressing toward the eschaton. Unlike the *aperion*, which resided outside of history, Yahweh acted and worked *within* history.

Whereas the Greek mind thingified the world, the Hebrew mind eventified it. If the world was space to the Greeks, it was time to the Hebrews. Reconciling these two fundamentally irreconcilable worldviews has become the identity project of the West for a little over the past two-thousand years. This project began when Greek-speaking Jewish scholars who were sequestered in the Jewish quarter of Alexandria, translated the Torah from its original Hebrew into *Koine*, a basic form of Greek, at the request of Ptomely II during the middle of the third century BC. The product of their collective efforts was the Septuagint. Creating the Septuagint was a practical act, since most Jews at that point in history had lost their Hebrew tongue and were speaking either Greek or Aramaic. It made sense to make the Torah accessible to the Jewish diaspora via the lingua franca of a Hellenistic world built by the conquests of Alexander the Great.

One unforeseen effect of the Septuagint was the Christ movement some three centuries after the translation was completed. The Septuagint allowed the Christ movement to leap the psychological chasm from Jew to gentile; enabling Paul of Tarsus and the evangelist Luke to bring Jewish thinking and feeling to non-Jewish audiences. The gentiles they wrote and preached to spoke Greek and viewed the world in essentially Greek ways. Greek became the written language of all forms of early Christianity and the linguistic vehicle for the early Christian movements of Gnosticism, Hermeticism, and eventually the canonized texts of the New Testament.

The creation of the Septuagint was the first time that the sacred Hebrew text was translated into another language. This was a monumental moment because the process of translation projected the original Hebrew outlook through the Greek linguistic prism. This act initiated marital union between their respective metaphysics—Greek space and Hebrew time—a process that reached its culmination a little over two-thousand years later (in 1907) when Hermann Minkowski, teacher of Albert Einstein, showed a geometric depiction of space-time as a fourth dimension, declaring that "from now onwards, space by itself and time by itself will recede completely to become mere shadows and only a type of union of the two will still stand independently on its own."[5]

CHAPTER 16:

The Lord of the East

When they cry to Yahweh for help because of oppressors,
he will send them a savior and leader to deliver them.

~ Isaiah 19:20

The Greeks and the Hebrews were unlikely bedfellows. Neither became aware of the existence of the other until the fourth century BC, when the son of a Macedonian king led his armies across the Ecumene.

With the end of the Third Sacred War in 346 BC, King Phillip II brought the bulk of the Greek Peninsula and the Balkans under Macedonian control, forming a sphere of Greek influence held together by Greek religion, language, and politics. The independent and still powerful city-states of Athens and Thebes feared the increasing power of the Macedonian ruler. In 340 BC, Athens violated the terms of the treaty imposed on her after its defeat during the Third Sacred War. By the middle of the following year, Phillip marched an army into southern Greece, prompting a hurried Greek alliance led by Athenian and Theban power. When the two sides met in 338 BC at Chaeronea, Macedonian forces crushed the Greeks, thanks largely to the tactical brilliance of Phillip's eighteen-year-old son, Alexander.

With the Athenians and Thebans defeated, Phillip II consolidated his power and set his sights on the Persian Empire. But the new leader of the Greek world would never see it fall.

Scarcely two years after his victory at Chaeronea, an assassin's blade cut him down. His successor, a now twenty-year-old Alexander, found himself at the head of the Corinthian League, an assembly of Greek city-states formed by Phillip after Chaeronea. After shoring up power back home and suppressing a Theban uprising in brutal fashion, Alexander marched into Asia in 334 BC and began a six-year campaign against the indomitable Persian Empire.

The handsome, clean-shaven[i] youth conquered Asia Minor, Syria-Palestine (the Levant), Egypt, Mesopotamia, and finally Persia itself over the course of four years. In Asia Minor, he routed the Persian king's satraps at the Battle of Granicus. Alexander then pushed south in Syria and defeated the king himself, Darius III, at the Battle of Issus, forcing the ruler to flee. Rather than take up chase, Alexander moved south and took Egypt in 332 BC, accepting Pharaoh's crown and elevation to divine status from the Egyptians, who called him the "Son of God."

Before leaving Egypt to resume his pursuit of Darius, Alexander ordered the construction of a city at the mouth of the Nile river that he would name *Alexandria*—the first city of many either established or renamed in honor of the self-declared Lord of Asia. Alexander then plunged into the heart of the Persian Empire. He defeated Darius again at the Battle of Guagamela in 331 BC and sacked the Persian capital, Persepolis, in 330 BC. Probably as revenge for the burning of the Athenian acropolis a century and a half before, Persepolis was looted and torched by Alexander's armies. As for the desperate Darius, he was betrayed by his own bodyguards who stabbed him and left him for dead. According to Alexander, when he found Darius, the ruler begged him to avenge him and even named him his successor.

---

[i] Alexander's beardless face became a masculine aesthetic ideal that is with us even today. The clean-shaven style is a standard across modern Western business professionals, politicians, and military men.

But Alexander was not satisfied with Persia. After spending the next two years cleaning up the remaining Persian resistance, he led his forces east into the Hindu Kush and put together a string of victories over a number of regional kings. But after one particularly costly battle at Hydaspes in 326 BC, the Greek forces under Alexander had had enough. They did not share their king's desire to conquer the known world (which for the Greeks ended somewhere at the eastern edge of India). The exhausted soldiers yearned for home and family and upon reaching the western bank of the River Hyphasis, refused to march further. Alexander was forced to turn back. He swung around the southern edge of Pakistan and forced a sixty-day march through the Gedrosian desert, emerging out of the hellish oven with one quarter of his army and leaving behind, if ancient reports are to be believed, a trail of some ninety-thousand bodies.

After returning to Persia, Alexander's health began to decline. He became paranoid and was often drunk. His adoption of Eastern customs and dress lost him the trust of the Macedonians at court. The death of Hephaestion, his closest friend and possible lover, in the year before his own demise, devastated Alexander and worsened his increasingly precarious mental state.

Despite his health issues, Alexander still made big plans. He would invade the Arabian Peninsula first and then crush that upstart of Latin farmers in Italy, then dismantle the powerful Carthaginians and expand his power to the western edges of Europe. One can only wonder what the cultural landscape of the world would look like today had both Arabia and Rome been subjugated by the Greeks under Alexander's rule. In June of 323 BC, as Alexander was mustering a massive force in Babylon for his invasion of the Arabian Peninsula, he fell ill and died at the age of thirty-two.

Alexander's plans died with him. No expansion into Arabia or the western Mediterranean ever happened. Any potential immediate successors among family and campaign companions were killed. His empire was divided up among a group of second-tier military officers into four factions: Ptolemy took Egypt and the Levant (which would change hands to the Seleucids over a century later), Antigonus II settled for Macedon and Greece, Seleucus took control of a vast swath of territory from the southern strip of Asia Minor to the Indus valley, while Lysimachus established reign over the majority of Asia Minor. For the next few centuries, these fiefdoms would fight each other and outside enemies until their absorption toward the end of the millennium by the Romans from the west and the Parthians, a revival of Persian power, from the east. Before their ultimate dissolution, however, Alexander's successor kingdoms injected a Greek outlook into the territories they ruled.

Alexander's death technically marks the end of the Classical Era and the beginning of the Hellenistic Period, a time of great Greek cultural expansion throughout much of the known world. Alexander himself was a catalyst for this. Greek culture was baked into his psyche. When he was thirteen, Aristotle was employed as his tutor. Alexander learned Greek and used it to conduct all formal administrative procedures. He always kept a copy of the *Illiad* with him, admiring and modeling himself after its hero, Achilles. Out of political shrewdness, Alexander encouraged intermarriage between Greeks, Egyptians, Persians, and Indians and cultural openness among his officers and administrators, but he ultimately loved Greek culture and poured it over the territories he conquered, leaving a trail of *gymnasiums*, Greek temples, Alexandrias, and *acras* from the Aegean to Egypt to the Indus Valley.

Spreading Greek culture was practical because it supported the administrative efforts of Alexander and his successor kingdoms. As a means of melding a collective religious consciousness together, Greek priests opened temple doors to locals and encouraged them to worship their own gods at its altars. The imposing *acras* housed Greek military garrisons, mixed speakers of Greek into the local population, and discouraged insurgencies. The *gymnasiums* allowed common people to exercise nude and take lessons from Greek philosophers, which in turn encouraged Greek thinking and promoted a Greek way of life. A Greek common tongue evolved as well, called *Koine. Koine* became the lingua franca of the post-Alexandrine world, used for commerce, trading, religious procedures, political administration, military operations, and everyday life. If you wanted to get around, you needed to know some Greek.

When Alexander marched through the Levant after beating Darius III the first time, he either failed to notice the Hebrews at all or never bothered to mention them. The Hebrews, on the other hand, may have quietly celebrated him if only because he relieved them of Persian rule. Situated in Judea during the Hellenistic Period, the Hebrews were first ruled by the Ptolemaics and then fell under the suzerainty of the Seleucids during the third century BC. By this point the Hebrews were accustomed to a revolving door of external rulers. First it was the Assyrians who toppled the Davidic Kingdom in the eighth century BC, then the Babylonians in the sixth, followed by the Persians later that same century, and then the Greeks.

The Macedonian Seleucids were less motivated by conquest than was Alexander. They needed to consolidate, administrate, and control their domain, not conquer the world. At first, the Seleucids made seemingly benign adjustments to Judea. The gymnasium they constructed in Jerusalem attracted many Jews, who saw the practical benefits of assimilating to a Greek way of life. And why not? For the Jews, this was, after all, the new world order of the Seleucids, who did not appear to be going anywhere anytime soon.

But the Seleucids pushed their Hellenization efforts too far. Their king, Antiochus IV Epiphanes, coveted the riches housed inside the Jewish temple. During the second quarter of the second century BC, he built an imposing *acra* next to it, erected a bronze statue of Zeus on the Jewish temple's altar, and forbade Jewish religious practice.

The Jews revolted. Although outnumbered, they defeated the Seleucids under the leadership of Judas Maccabeus. They restored the temple, stripped it of the taint of Antiochus, and gained back a respectable measure of self-sovereignty. But as successful as the Maccabees were, they lacked the numbers to overthrow the Seleucids entirely. Still contained within the Seleucid Empire and ultimately subordinate to them, they nonetheless carved out a semi-independent state and were finally at least administrated by one of their own.

The Maccabean successors, the Hasmoneans, oversaw Judea in cahoots with their Seleucid superiors. They would continue this administrative model through their last dynastic line (the Herods) as Judea fell into Roman hands and became one of its client states in 63 BC. In exchange for letting a Jew rule Judea, the imperialists, whether of the Greek or Roman strain, demanded a steady stream of taxes, which the Hasmoneans were all too willing to provide by tightly controlling and monetizing temple procedures.

An unfortunate repeated historical occurrence is that after most successful revolutions, the bureaucrats tasked with ruling the prize won by their zealous predecessors fall short of living up to the original, revolutionary vision. This case was no different. The vision of the Maccabees was quickly shelved by the Hasmoneans, whose interest in power and wealth outstripped revolutionary idealism or devotion to Yahweh's law. To many Jews, the Hasmoneans were corrupt, greedy businessmen whose political collusion with outsiders and racketeering of the temple amounted to nothing less than blasphemy. No shock that by the turn of the millennium, radical anti-establishment groups like the Zealots and the Essenes appeared. One associate of both was a man born in Bethlehem in 4 BC.

Jesus's calls for bringing the Kingdom of God to Earth were on some level geopolitical. He wanted to overthrow Rome and opposed the authority of the Pharisees and the Sadducees, the Jewish religious elite, who mediated the relationship between the Jews and the local Roman administrators. According to some scholars, the claim of Jesus's revolutionary intent is vindicated by the style of his execution, which under Roman law was exclusively reserved for those who committed acts of sedition and treason.[ii] Although establishing the historical context surrounding him is important, we must set aside the historical Jesus for now. We will turn to Christ the myth and its psychological implication for the West in the next chapter.

ii For more information on this perspective, see Reza Aslan, *Zealot: The Life and Times of Jesus of Nazareth*, (New York: Random House, 2013).

CHAPTER 17:

The God-Man

I am an historian, I am not a believer, but I must confess as a historian that this penniless preacher from Nazareth is irrevocably the very center of history.

~ H.G. Wells

The Self's conscious incarnation into human form was a gradual process played out between God and man throughout the Old Testament. In Genesis, the Self incarnates in Adam the Anthropos, the man who becomes ego-aware yet remains unconscious of his relationship to the Self. In this case, God is unconscious of its own totality from the standpoint of its Adam incarnation—an incomplete incarnation to be sure. As the Old Testament progresses, God's awareness of itself through man grows through a series of events—the Voice's contact with Avraham in Harran, the reversal of the age-old custom of human sacrifice in the story of his son Yitzhak,[i] Yahweh's confrontation with Moshe through the burning bush, Yahweh's encounter with Job—and climaxes with Christ, the incarnation fully aware of its dual God-man nature.

In one way, Christ is typical. He is like every cosmic hero. The structure of his myth follows a pattern similar to Gilgamesh, Sargon, Oedipus, Moshe, Heracles, Cyrus, and many others. The

[i] There are two instances of human sacrifice that occur in the Old Testament, both under morally depraved circumstances (Kings 16: 2-3 and Judges 11: 29-40). Neither instance was ordered by Yahweh.

modes of worship of Christ's early followers were influenced by the pre-existent Orphic mysteries and the contemporary cults of Mithras and Dionysus. But on the other hand, no other figure occupies more space in the Western mind than Christ. Whether believer or nonbeliever, everyone in the West knows the name "Jesus." Compared to all other mythic heroes of Western history, Christ sits in a class of his own.

The reason for this is because the Christ-figure is the unique result of a combined Judeo-Greco metaphysic. Christ is the cosmic coordination of divine space and time, the embodied Self fully aware of itself in the world.[1] Notice that the phrase *Jesus of Nazareth* automatically connects his person to a specific location on Earth. Boman points this out:

> "In the revelation of God in Christ, there is not only a divine *Now* but also a divine *Here*; together they form the hard reality. It is one-sided to designate the revelation of God only as historical; just as characteristic of God's revelation in Christ is that it unfolded in the material world spatially, visibly, and palpably."[2]

With the inclusion of the Greek outlook in Hebrew psychology, the incarnation of God into man did not just happen some*time*, it happened some*where*. The eternal divine that exists beyond the material world (Greek-Platonic), and the God that works *within* time moving mankind toward a goal (Hebrew-Eschatological), coalesce together to become the Christ-figure. It is no surprise that in Christian tradition, Jesus's preaching—the heard—is just as central to his identity and divinity as his material substance, his body and blood—the seen—sacrificed for the redemption of man's tumble into ego-hood. By uniting the Judeo and Greco perspectives and the case-limits of their respective ideals, it became possible, indeed inevitable, for God to manifest in both space *and* time.

Christ can be said to be the Hellenistic interpretation of the Hebrew God incarnated as *both* image and word, or *Logos*. From a Greek perspective, Christ is the miraculous action of the Platonic Intellect, the *Logos*, projecting into three-dimensional *space*, becoming a material being, and subjecting itself to the corrupting hand of time. From the Judeo metaphysical standpoint, Christ represents the fulfillment of an *event*, the Old Testament revelation process of the coming of the Son of Man. This gives new meaning as to why the West's Julian and Gregorian calendrical systems designate Christ's life as the cornerstone of time itself; BC counts down to AD—*Anno Domini*, which means "the Year of Our Lord."[ii] —because Christ is the cosmic Now. "I am the alpha and the omega, the first and the last, the beginning and the end." (Rev. 22:13)

The Self and ego interface consciously as Christ, neither one unconscious of the other. "I and the Father are one" (John 10:30). Christ is the complete image of man for the West, the hero who is *both* man and God, the psychological center of mass, whose gravity anchors each ego of Western origin. Every ego of Christian background constellates back to the central Christ-figure. It represents the supreme individual. When schizophrenics break away from sanctioned reality, they sometimes realize they are Christ incarnate, or at least embodiments of his fated return. They do not think this. They *know* it, whether they're religiously inclined or not. The mythology of Christ gives them a symbolic framework through which they become conscious of the mystery of somehow being *both* God and mortal human. This experience flabbergasts Western egos because knowing that you are God is the West's best-kept psychological secret.

[ii] The term *Anno Dominus*, which translates to "in the year of our Lord" (AD), was conceived in the sixth century by Dionysus Exiguus.

Even to a twenty-first-century mind, announcing that you are God is a kind of modern blasphemy, one treated with antipsychotics and padded rooms (as opposed to the older methods of exile, torture, or execution). This taboo exists for the good reason of protecting against ego inflation. The mythological structure of the Abrahamic religions acts as a safety lock on an ego that otherwise can and does blow through its boundaries and identify *as* Self, which is an unsustainable psychological state to occupy. John Doe and Jane Smith are masks the Self puts on; they are not the Self.

But Westerners living in an age in which their dominant myth lies shattered in a heap of broken images, risk a solipsistic, ego-inflated state. They may feel convinced that their personality is the controller of reality—a personality that is maybe even entitled to fealty and worship. This is a God-complex, and a dangerous psychological state. Strip a person with a Judeo-Christian upbringing of their religious structure, turn them nihilist, and the risk of inflation increases.

Part of this problem has to do with how the West sees God. To the West, God is the creator-ruler of nature. God is an individual. To the East, God is both nature and man. God is non-individual. The Chinese word for nature is *ziran* (自然), which means "so-of-itself." Whereas the Abrahamic God makes and controls nature, the East's Tao or Brahman self-organizes *as* nature. The West, in contrast to the East, identifies strongly with the individual. In its normal state, the Westernized ego verges on over-inflation. Nowhere else do personality cults thrive like they do in the West. Whether it's Alexander the Great, Julius Caesar, Saint Augustine of Hippo, Leonardo Da Vinci, Martin Luther, Voltaire, Adolf Hitler, Joseph Stalin, Donald Trump, or Elon Musk, the work, feats, accomplishments, blunders, and humiliations of famous men are intimately bound up with their identities. Sociopathic, modern masters of Wall Street or narcissistic personalities are byproducts of the egoistic over-inflation urge.

The personality cult of Kim Il Sung, late head of the ruling dynasty of North Korea, is a case-in-point example of the inflated, tyrannical God-complex. It has the state of North Korea fully in its grip. The mythos underlying the ruling structure of North Korea is biblical. Kim Il Sung's family were deeply religious Presbyterian Christians. In North Korean culture, Kim Il Sung is both God and man. He is the supreme individual, who, instead of conducting individuality to his populace, deprives them of it. According to the North Korean refugee Yeonmi Park, time began when Kim II Sung was born, and each citizen of the socialist paradise was made in his image. The North Koreans apparently have no word for *I*, and the only kind of love admissible in their language is love for Kim Il Sung. Although Kim Il Sung is dead, it is commonly known that he is aware of everything you do, every thought you have, and as Luke the evangelist noted about Christ, he numbers the hairs on your head down to their last.[iii]

The danger of ego-inflation in the East has traditionally been less than it is in the West. In the East it is mythologically permissible for each person to be an incarnation of the Godhead. The core mantra of the Upanishads is public knowledge: *tat tvam asi*, "Thou art That," or "You are the One." Perhaps this is another strategy for preventing egoistic over-inflation. Instead of acting like a pressure lock, as it does in the West, the myth structure in the East is a pressure *release*. Rather than seal the ego into a container and isolate it from knowledge of God, the East allows the ego to rest in homeostatic equilibrium with the Self. Making the divine nature of each person plainly known, equalizes everyone. Unlike the myths of the West, the myths

[iii] If further interested, the reader is encouraged to read *In Order to Live: A North Korean Girl's Journey to Freedom*, by Yeonmi Park and Maryanne Vollers (Baltimore: Penguin Books, 2016).

of the East *consciously* and overtly acknowledge the connection between ego and Self.

That is not to say that the mythology of the East is right and the West is wrong. Both fit the psychological needs of their people. We must compare them side-by-side to become aware of their assumptions. One instructive way to do this is to look at their central figures.

Christ's Eastern counterpart is the Buddha. Siddhartha Guatama lived about five-hundred years before Christ and was born in Lumbini in southern Nepal. Unlike the lowly-born Jesus, Siddhartha was an aristocrat. According to the legend, Siddhartha's father tried to retain him in the royal palace to prevent him from seeing the suffering of the world. But Siddhartha chose to go out and see it rather than remain in ignorance. In psychological terms, the Self, instead of staying unconscious in eternal undifferentiated bliss within itself—like Siddartha remaining safe and ignorant on royal grounds—manifests in the world as the ego and experiences suffering and death. It abandons its infinite nature for finitude.

Siddhartha toured the commons and saw misery, starvation, and suffering. One day, when meditating under a bodhi tree, he experienced mystical consciousness and became the Buddha, or "Awakened One." In his moment of enlightenment-ecstasy,[iv] he escaped the wheel of reincarnation or, said another way, transcended time into eternity, rose above ego-hood to Self-hood. From the standpoint of mystical consciousness, the ego died and the Self was made whole in a *coincidentia oppositorum*.

Notice the opposing quintessential images of Christ and Buddha. Whereas Buddha, son of a king, cuts an androgenous[v]

[iv] "Ecstatic" comes from the Greek word *existansai* which "means to displace, put outside of place, drive out of one's mind, stand outside of oneself" or *ekstasis* which means "entrancement, insanity, astonishment." See Online Etymology Dictionary, 2021, https://www.etymonline.com/word/ecstatic

[v] Many Buddhas of the Theravada and Mahayana traditions depict an androgynous figure. This symbolizes Buddha's resolution of duality.

(i.e. whole) regal figure, sitting cross-legged in tranquil bliss underneath the bodhi tree, Christ, son of a carpenter, is a peasant male; he hangs naked, his body tortured, limbs impaled on wooden beams. This is because Buddha represents the metaphysical union of the Self and ego from the perspective of the Self, while Christ represents the metaphysical union of the Self and ego from the perspective of the ego. Christ's suffering and death stands for the painful dissolution of the ego undergoing reunion with the Self. The initial panic and sense of annihilation that accompanies a near-death experience or a heroic dose of psychedelic drugs is the felt experience of psychological crucifixion. On the other hand, the picture-message of the Buddha—hermaphroditic, complete, sitting in ecstasy—symbolizes the Self's orgasmic reunion with itself following ego-annihilation. These are two related yet opposing perspectives on the same process.

Christ is the suffering servant, the lamb of God to be sacrificed. Whereas Buddha came from high royalty, Christ was a commoner, born where animals sleep. And unlike Buddha, Christ's mission is not to join the world, for he already exists within it as a mortal man of humble origins. His mission is to die and depart from the world, as a means of reunifying with God the Father (Self). Buddha chose to *enter* the world. Christ was born to *leave* it. Christ's act of self-sacrifice redeems man's soul from its long-ago fall into ego-consciousness. *Lamb of God, who takest away the sins of the world, grant us peace!*[vi] The lamb is sacrificed for the worldly sins—gluttony, pride, sloth, envy, lust, greed, wrath—all of which are unconscious patterns of addiction, each a form of painful over-involvement in the world of matter. By freeing ourselves of attachment, a misidentification with the phenomenal world, there is nothing left but peace granted to us underneath the bodhi tree.

[vi] This prayer comes from the Anglican *Book of Common Prayer*.

The image of a dying Christ reminds us that suffering is fundamental to existence, if not, as the Buddha discovered, the very nature of existence itself. Whereas Christ is the West's "consciousness as agony," Buddha is the East's "consciousness as tranquil bliss."[3] Brutally nailed to wood, Christ represents the Self's acceptance of its painful subjection to matter as the ego, while the calm, ecstatic Buddha represents the Self's blissful transcendence of the world. The West's scientific descent into matter and the East's study of the rhythms of eternity articulated in the *I Ching* are deeply connected to these respective worldviews. "United," Christ and Buddha "picture the two sides of the carrier of consciousness," matter versus form, time versus eternity, word versus image, left brain versus right brain, ego versus Self.[4] Each of us in mystical consciousness is a unification of Christ and Buddha.

PART III:
THE SIMULACRUM OF THE UNIVERSE

CHAPTER 18:

The Collapse of Civilization

The decline of Rome was the natural and inevitable effect of immoderate greatness. Prosperity ripened the principle of decay; the causes of destruction multiplied with the extent of conquest; and, as soon as time or accident had removed the artificial supports, the stupendous fabric yielded to the pressure of its own weight.

~ Edward Gibbon[i]

Nearly four-hundred years after the death of Jesus, Alaric, and his army of thirty-thousand Visigoths marched to Rome, parleyed with a few of its terrified officials, strode through its Salarian gates, and pillaged the city. The sun was setting on the Roman Empire, though this was not obvious to its inhabitants. To many of its citizens and deluded leaders, Rome was still the indomitable force it had always been. Irritating and wild barbarians sometimes tested its borders, and yes, they admitted, that was happening a bit more lately, but none would dare challenge the Eternal City itself, not since the Gauls had sacked it in 390 BC. But that was a long time ago. And everyone knew what Julius Caesar did to the Gauls.

It is difficult for any society, especially one beyond its prime, to face its problems honestly. It is easier to revel in

i See Edward Gibbon's *The History of the Decline and Fall of the Roman Empire*, vol. 6

past accomplishments, speak of founders long dead, surround oneself with sycophants, drape bleak realities in euphemisms, recite comforting cliches, and point fingers at scapegoats than it is to confront cracking infrastructure, corruption, and broken administrative models. Such was the case with fifth-century Rome. It was on the cusp of a dark age.

One of the primary factors in Rome's decline was the disappearance of its middle class, the *curiales*. The *curiales* were middle-scale landowners and Rome's primary tax base. They vanished gradually over the first few centuries of the Common Era, leaving only the tax-exempt rich and a poor underclass, who could not by themselves possibly finance Rome's interminable military operations abroad and its increasingly unmanageable border problems. The *curiales* were put in a double-bind. It was their duty by birth to collect taxes for the emperor, and each had a quota of taxes to collect. If the quota was not met, the difference came out of their own pockets. Originally their position in society was an honorable one because they were the municipal officials who supported the upkeep of the cities.

But as generations passed and tax obligations became more and more difficult to fulfill, the *curiales* tried to escape their class. Those who could, bought their way into political, military, or ecclesiastical office, while those who could not, traded in their birth assignment for other professions. These workarounds were eventually shut down by decree of the emperor. Many *curiales* had to borrow from the rich to stay afloat.

Rich landowners were only too happy to put the tax man in their debt, for this not only guaranteed exemption from taxation, but also guaranteed repossession of *curiales'* land and property after they defaulted. The problem of Rome's disappearing middle class became a runaway crisis. Not only was Rome's tax pool evaporating but so too the very people charged with civic building programs, infrastructure maintenance, and public services. As the *curiales* were swallowed up by the estates of the wealthy, infrastructure began to decay. Sewers stopped working, imports dried up, cisterns broke, and people just no longer showed up to fix these things. The gap between the rich and poor grew. Lack of class contact calcified social and bureaucratic divisions, which made systemic change impossible. Rome lost the ability to reform itself.

There was little the emperor could do to change much of anything. Toward Rome's final days, the emperor's power depended exclusively on a money-starved Roman military, which had become unreliable and perhaps too self-aware. Many emperors had been propped up or deposed by the army. And when the Roman army mandated recruits from the estates of the rich, many got away with sending money or slaves instead. In its final centuries, Rome's legions looked more barbarian than Roman. In the end, Rome was starved for conscripts, gold, and capable leadership.

Toward the end of the fifth century, proto-medieval society began to take shape amidst the crumbling Roman polis. Wealthy landowners had all but absorbed the middle class into their estates either as "freemen," skilled artisans loyal to the lord of the estate, or, for the more financially unfortunate, indebted serfs now bound to the land. Many of the former *curiales*, once respectable, literate members of society, degenerated into illiterate tenant farmers who paid tithes to the estate owner in exchange for protection from barbarian raids or rogue Roman military units. By the time the last Western Roman emperor died in 476 AD, highways were no longer safe. Goths and Vandals routinely pillaged and terrorized city and countryside alike.

But marauding was not the sole occupation of Europe's northern tribes, of course. Eager for the benefits of Roman civilization, many barbarian chiefs settled down into former empire territory as landowning farmers. They took on the religion and eventually the literacy of their Roman cultural superiors. These petty barbarian dominions mutated into the Christian fiefdoms of Charlemagne's age and into the powerful European kingdoms of the High Middle Ages.

But much was lost with the decline of Roman civilization. Life expectancy rates dropped; Latin died as a common tongue (though it did not go extinct); ideas and texts were scattered, forgotten, or destroyed wholesale; learning stagnated; literacy rates declined; and civil order became the exception rather than the rule. As we have pointed out, rule of law is an abstraction, a construct suited to the orientation of a society determined by left-brain values. As people gradually forgot how to read and write, the cognitive pendulum swung back toward the right-brain, making it nearly impossible to systemically maintain and enforce such collective abstractions. Tribal mores,[ii] rather than rule of law, held sway. The Western psyche had disintegrated.

There was, however, one tradition that remained standing amidst the ruins of Roman civilization: the office of the Catholic clergy. In many cases, the only leadership left after Roman imperial officials abandoned their posts was the Catholic bishop. They were the final remnants of the old-world order. Often the bishop and his scribes were the only literates among a community of serfs and petty, barbarian kings who could neither read nor write. Currency, book-keeping, law, mathematics, academia—these were *civilized* abstractions locked away behind the doors of literacy. The Catholic orthodoxy held the keys.

Christianity was a grassroots religion. It had arisen over the course of the first three centuries out of a smattering of loosely affiliated communities and churches sprinkled across the Roman Mediterranean. Common between them was a belief in the divine nature of Jesus Christ and that his return would bring about the end of the world. One bizarre rite many

---

[ii] E.g., chivalry

organizations practiced was the consumption of their God-man. But beyond a few core principles, many Christian sects had their own customs and cosmic interpretations informed by their pagan backgrounds. The Christian Manichees, for example, banned reproduction because it perpetuated the entrapment of divine spirit inside of matter. The Platonic distrust of matter/flesh formed a vital part of the Christian heart. The Manichees believed that spirit was inherently good and matter was evil. God was good but not omnipotent because omnipotence would make God responsible for the evil in the world. Their founder Mani was a Parthian who was undoubtedly influenced by Persian dualism.

At first, the absence of a unified set of beliefs and customs across Christian sects was not an issue. For any eschatological cult, why build bureaucracy or campaign for a common doctrine when the end is nigh? But this lack of structure was to become a nagging problem for the Christian movement, especially as two things became clear. First, Christ's return and the end of the world did not seem as historically imminent as originally anticipated. Second, Roman power was falling apart. Who was going to maintain law and order? Who was going to keep records and administrate? Who would keep the community safe from raiders? Christianity not only lacked the administrative structure to address practical issues of shelter and security, but also the uniform ethos and identity to provide a standardized set of answers to religious questions. One need not look further than Paul's letters to the Galatians during the first century and his frustrations therein to see the beginnings of what was to become, by the third century, a mass movement struggling to agree on what it was.

By the beginning of the fourth century, Christianity was legalized by Emperor Constantine and became the official religion of the Roman world. Soon after its legalization, its core beliefs were codified by a meeting of bishops at the western edge of Asia in the city of Nicaea in 325 AD. The bishops gathered at the behest of Constantine to establish consensus on the interpretations of the divine nature of the Son of God and his metaphysical relationship to God the Father. The Council of Nicaea was an important stage in the history of the Catholic Church, in part because it signaled the end of any grassroots, democratic promise the movement once had. The attending bishops had come from a long line of people, *both* men and women in the early days, who administered and organized churches at the pleasure of and for their local congregations. The early Catholic bishop was elected by his or her people. But by the fourth century, election was the exception. The bishops who attended Constantine's first ecumenical council in Nicaea virtually all appointed each other, as Catholic bishops have done ever since.

When looked at in terms of pure causality, it is difficult to understand how the offshoot of an upstart, monotheistic religion in some backwater of the Roman Empire took the polytheistic minds and hearts of the West's largest civilization by storm in just three-hundred years. This transformation is even harder to understand when you consider that the Christian movement was at first openly persecuted and suppressed by the Roman state. The Church's central figure along with many of its later disciples and leaders were routinely martyred in brutal fashion. But the mass conversion of the Greco-Roman world to Christianity becomes easier to understand when looked at from a psychohistorical perspective.

Although worship of Greek and Roman gods continued until the middle of the first millennium AD, as early as the fifth century BC its practice had become a public exercise and was understood foremost as a mechanism of social union and administration. As the Greco-Roman psyche organized—in other words, as it became more ego-conscious—the archetypal gods and goddesses came to seem less relevant. Observance of the Indo-European pantheon puttered out, and Greco-Roman consciousness hungrily absorbed a quasi-Jewish religion in the younger and more vigorous form of Christianity, whose monotheistic structure corresponded to and resonated with an increasingly ego-conscious society.

CHAPTER 19:

Saint Augustine: Prototype for Western Man

So in the flash of a trembling glance, it attained to that which is. At that moment I saw your 'invisible nature understood through the things which are made.'

~ *Saint Augustine*[1]

There was probably no man more aware of his ego in the late Greco-Roman world than Augustine of Hippo (354–430 AD). He was a Christian convert whose mind shaped the Western psyche. He wrote history's first genuine autobiography, *Confessions*. No work of its like existed before this time because no one was self-reflecting in the way Augustine was. Recalling his twenties, Augustine confesses to us:

> "In those years I had a woman. She was not my partner in what is called a lawful marriage. I had found her in my state of wandering desire and lack of prudence. Nevertheless, she was the only girl for me, and I was faithful to her. With her I learned by direct experience how wide a difference there is between the partnership of marriage entered into for the sake of having a family and the mutual consent of those whose love is a matter of physical sex, and for whom the birth

> of a child is contrary to their intention—even though, if offspring arrive, they compel their parents to love them."[2]

Many of us know well, on the one hand, a person we've hotly burned for who never fully leaves our heart, and, on the other hand, a person with whom we've gradually built love over time and whose steady company aligns more practically with our professional and private trajectories.

On the sudden death of his best friend, Nebridus, Augustine falls into a depression we can relate to:

> "I was surprised that any other mortals were alive, since he whom I had loved as if he would never die, was dead. I was even more surprised that when he was dead I was still alive, for he was 'my other self'...So I boiled with anger, sighed, wept, and was at my wits' end. I found no calmness, no capacity for deliberation. I carried my lacerated and bloody soul when it was unwilling to be carried by me. I found no place where I could put it down. There was no rest in pleasant groves, nor in games or songs, nor in sweet-scented places, nor in exquisite feasts, nor in the pleasures of the bedroom and bed, nor, finally in book and poetry. Everything was an object of horror, even light itself; all that was not he, made me feel sick and was repulsive—except for groaning and tears."[3]

When Nebridus died, a part of Augustine died as well. Nothing he tried brought any reprieve to his grief. The astounding part of Augustine's story is that in it we find a person who, despite existing sixteen-hundred years apart from us, feels eerily contemporaneous with ourselves.

We see the word *I* appearing in literature before Augustine's *Confessions,* but not in the way in which Augustine uses it. Never had *I* been so personal, so frequent, so self-absorbed, so self-reflective, so tortured by self-consciousness, and so like ourselves as it was with Augustine. Today, we are accustomed to the personal in everything. Nothing holds our attention and touches us as solidly as the personal narrative. We demand it from almost every movie, book, advertisement, and television show. But in the ancient and classical worlds, this was not the case. Again, Cahill: "Open any collections of Great Thoughts or Great Sayings and let your eye pick out the *I*'s. In the oldest literature, their paucity and lack of force will begin to impress you...personal revelation, such as we are utterly accustomed to, is nowhere to be found." Even the meditations of Marcus Aurelius from the second century "for all their ponderousness... are never more personal than a Chinese fortune cookie."[4]

Augustine surprises us with a quality of self-loathing matched only perhaps by a modern:

> "I did not wish to observe myself, and you [God] set me before my face so that I should see how vile I was, how twisted and filthy, covered in sores and ulcers. And I looked and was appalled, but there was no way of escaping myself...you thrust me before my own eyes so that I should discover my iniquity and hate it."[5]

Cahill reminds us that "No one had ever talked this way before. If we page quickly through world literature from its beginnings to the advent of Augustine, we realize that with Augustine human consciousness takes a quantum leap forward—and becomes self-consciousness."[6] Reflecting intensely enough to experience and then pour one's inner turmoil onto paper in vivid detail, or to weigh the good and bad things we have done in our lives, is a state of consciousness that we take for granted. We live in an age that enables and indeed encourages such frames of mind.

The early Church, so deeply influenced by the Neo-Platonism and Stoicism conferred through Plotinus, Philo Judaeus, and Augustine, sanctified the realms of form and spirit (left brain) while tending to degrade the embodied, the material, the flesh (right brain). Heaven was nowhere to be found in the stinking world of matter. That we find ourselves in this realm of corruption and decay must be a mistake.

Augustine concluded that this mistake was made by Adam in the Garden of Eden. Original Sin, a concept that he extrapolated out of one of Paul's letters to the early church in Rome,[i] was a sin "which dwelt in me."[7] This inner sin was Adam's eating of the forbidden fruit. And it was inherited by all of mankind. To Augustine, Adam was that human "in whom we all died and from whom we were all born into a condition of misery."[8] At first glance, this seems like one of history's biggest guilt trips (and indeed was interpreted as such by the Augustinian Calvinists over a thousand years later), but if looked at psychologically, Augustine's point is about the ego. Augustine is tortured by ego-consciousness, by the split in his psyche:

> "As I deliberated about serving my Lord God, the self which willed to serve was identical with the self which was unwilling. It was I. I was neither wholly willing nor wholly unwilling. So I was in conflict with myself and was dissociated from myself. The dissociation came about against my will. Yet this was not a manifestation of the nature of an alien mind but the punishment suffered in my own mind…the

[i] Original Sin was a construct of Saint Augustine's mind. There is no mention of it in Genesis or the rest of the Bible.

> punishment of a more freely chosen sin, because I was a son of Adam."[9]

With deep self-psychoanalytic aptitude, Augustine recognized the conscious/unconscious, Self/ego schizophrenia in his own mind. Augustine's insistence on the collective inheritance of one man's sin by all mankind makes more sense when understood psychologically and mythologically. Adam is the figurative symbol by which man meets with and understands his own mortality; he is the man in whom we all die. Adam represents our recognition that we have fallen out of eternity into time, out of our eternal psychological union with God in Eden into ego-hood and all of its attendant desires and concerns. In him, civilized man's inner contradictions between I and thou, gain and loss, beginning and end, birth and death clash.

Saint Augustine was a father of Catholic orthodoxy and paved the way for medieval thinking. Before his conversion to orthodox Catholicism, Augustine was a Manichaean with neoplatonic roots. He attempted to reconcile the dualisms of body/flesh, spirit/matter, and form/content within the Christian mind. But Augustine trusted his left brain more than his right. He favored the abstract over the concrete, spirit over matter, form over content, mind over body. He conferred this bias to Christian thinking, leading to its distrust of the human body and its restrictive attitudes toward sex.

Augustine was the culmination of an evolving ego-consciousness in the ancient mind, the last of its kind. He is considered by many to be the prototypical modern man. Shortly after his death in 430 AD, Rome breathed its last and Europe began to shift into an unconscious state. Not until after the Dark Ages will we see the resurrection of *I* and its viral proliferation at the historic intersection of the Renaissance, the Protestant Reformation, and the printing press.

CHAPTER 20:

Medieval Mary: An Interval of Unconsciousness

Before the lights of literacy went out, the Christian orthodox leaders—Paul, Tertullian, Jerome, and Augustine—had hammered together a religion whose central themes were sin, guilt, and suffering. When the lights came on again in the tenth century, Europeans had leavened these with an increased respect for birth and womanhood. This revised ethos changed the character of Christianity and is best illustrated by the sharp and unexpected ascendance of Marianism...Unlike Jesus, the Dark Age Mary rarely speaks...her subjects came to know her through her image...the likeness of the Blessed Mother became ubiquitous throughout Western Europe.

~ Leonard Shlain[1]

The Medieval Era was an interim period, the unconscious interval between Classical Rome and the Modern Period. It is divided into three segments: the Dark Ages or Early Middle Ages (400–1100 AD), the High Middle Ages (1100–1350 AD), and the Late Middle Ages (1350–1492 AD).

Ego-consciousness in the West, previously well-established during the Greco-Roman period, collectively disintegrated during the Dark Ages. Libraries were destroyed; Plato,

Aristotle, Demosthenes, Homer, Virgil, and Cicero were lost, and the fires of learning put out. The Western psyche shifted toward right-brain holism. As the Greek East retreated into the safety of tradition and conservatism, the Latin West had to somehow absorb the pagan Germanic, Slavic, and Celtic tribes pouring across western Rome's borders and incorporate their theological multiplicity into a monotheistic consciousness without compromising the triune model of Christianity: the Father, Son and Holy Ghost.

One of the unifying characteristics of preliterate pagan culture was the elevated status of its women compared to the literate Greco-Romans, whose women as a rule stood without much remark in the anteroom of history. Preliterate cultures also worshiped and revered images, another contradiction the Catholic Church had to somehow reconcile with its iconophobic Judaic roots.

As pagan tribes merged with the Latin West, collective expression swung back toward image. Feminine symbolism resurged. Images were sanctioned by Pope Gregory the Great, who at the end of the sixth century lifted the stricture of the commandment against "graven images," declaring that "painting can do for the illiterate what writing does for those who can read."[2] Many paintings of the time focused on Mary, mother of Jesus, who was in the preceding age virtually unaccounted for by the fathers of orthodox Christianity. Augustine, Jerome, Paul of Tarsus, and the Evangelists of the New Testament scarcely mention her. When Pope Gregory the Great commissioned the first painting of the Catholic Church, it was of him receiving a blessing from none other than the Virgin Mary herself.[3]

The prominence of medieval Mary neared that of the Great Goddess of the Neolithic and Paleolithic ages. Once a lowly peasant girl of Nazareth, Mary joined a class of goddesses that included the ancient Inanna, Nut, Astarte, and Isis, when Mary received the honorific title of Queen of Heaven sometime near the turn of the first millennium. Some thousand years later, her assumption into Heaven would be officially admitted into church doctrine by Pope Pius XII. And like her prehistoric and ancient prefigures, Mary was depicted, not described. She *appeared* to her devotees as *image*, unlike Yahweh who *spoke* to his elect through *word*. Devotion to Mary was expressed not through script but through paintings, stained glass, or stone. She was often symbolized as the rose or the lily, its open petals forming a passive receptacle, symbol of man's feminine half.[4] That one of the primary myths of the Dark Ages centered on retrieving the supreme symbol of the feminine—the Holy Grail[i]—is not coincidence.

If the ancient Greek world was one of left-brain abstraction, the medieval Latin world was one of right-brain images. The rise of feminine reverence in medieval Europe seems peculiar on the surface because we find barely a whisper of it in the Greco-Roman tradition, nor much of it in the Judaic tradition either. And although we find evidence of the cult of the Virgin as early as the late second century (in images of her inscribed above the tombs of early Christians), signs of worship of Mary would not become obvious until the fifth century in Rome (in the Basilica of Santa Maria in Trastevere, the earliest church dedicated to Mary).

Many ancient pagan holy sites across the Mediterranean were also rededicated to Mary during this time, including the Parthenon of Athena. And virtually all of the great gothic cathedrals erected during the High Middle Ages were dedicated to Mary—most notably the Notre Dame cathedral in France. One important twelfth century image shows us a turning point in sacred art in the apse of Mary of Trastevere. Here we find Mary shown as seated on the throne of mercy next to Jesus her son, who has his arm wrapped around her in a display of

---

[i] The pursuit of the Holy Grail—the chalice from which Jesus, according to legend, drank at the Last Supper—formed the central quest of Celtic Christendom during the Medieval Period.

affection unprecedented in religious art of the time. The drab, abstract, left brain of the orthodox Greek East has finally given way to the color, emotion, and earthiness of the right brain in this striking image. Cahill excitedly describes the moment:

> "Anatomically, kinetically, instinctively this is an entirely novel moment in the history of sacred art... By this single gesture, Western art is freed from its Eastern enchantment. The long tradition of representing spirit by super-serious faces and two-dimensional, stick-figure human bodies starved, denatured, aloof, and devoid of movement, is about to give way, as Western Europeans discover a new embodiment, a new earthiness, a new bounce—a new kind of Heaven."[5]

Abstraction, a specialty of the left brain, corresponds to spirit and sky, while concretism, the specialty of the right brain, corresponds to matter and earth. Traditional Church art that came out of the literate, static, intermittently iconoclastic East was reluctant to show human feeling and bodily substance, instead preferring solemn, rigid faces disinterested in the world. But the mosaic of Mary of Trastavere shows us a change in the European mind.

Cahill is right. For the medieval mind, this *was* a new kind of Heaven. Heaven, in the essence of Mary, was conceived not as some cold, abstract, Platonic, extra-dimensional realm for the soul to flee to after death, but as a place warm with the colors, beauty, senses, and emotions of the Earth. It was the world itself, the embodied, the domain of the Goddess. It was the loving embrace between a mother and her son.

And although the image resurged in the Middle Ages, the personal did not. During historical intervals, ego-centricity plummets alongside literacy while unconscious egalitarian values ascend. When this happens, people are depicted, if at all, in archetypal fashion. Images of the divine may emerge, but not pictures of the personal. Medieval people, in the art of the era, are typically portrayed without unique, identifying features. They are flattened out into universal, generalized images.

> "Though there had been portraits in the classical period—we have a pretty good idea, for instance, of what Socrates, Plato, Alexander, and the Caesars looked like—we have none to speak of from the long Middle Ages. Hildegard's portrait, perhaps even drawn by her, is just the Typical Nun. Similarly, the few appearances of Queen Eleanor in paint are of the Typical Queen. There may be one genuine likeness of Francis of Assisi, a homely little fellow painted by Cimabue; all the other dozens of depictions of Francis are simply the Typical Heroic Male Saint of the period."[6]

Consciousness, during the darker intervals of history, is less...well, self-conscious.

CHAPTER 21:

Man, the Measure of All Things

Eternity is called whole, not because it has parts, but because it is lacking in nothing.

~ Saint Thomas Aquinas[1]

When literacy reemerged in Europe, it linearized the European mind. Europe began to reconstruct a historical image of itself. It reached back one-thousand years to its nearly forgotten Greco-Roman worldview and began to revive the aesthetics, values, and modes of thought from that era. This time, instead of the drama of Zeus and Athena and Jove and Romulus, a Greco-Roman lens would be used to portray the stories and images from the Bible. The Sistine Chapel ceiling, Dante's tour of the inferno, and the various sculptures of David from Donatello to Michelangelo, reflect a European mind in the process of reviving its Greco-Roman past and submerging it in Judeo-Christian thinking and feeling.

Greek ways of scientific thought were resurrected by great medieval thinkers like Thomas Aquinas and Roger Bacon during the thirteenth century. Thanks to Islamic scholars in Arabia who maintained relationships with the Byzantines in the Greek East, Aristotle's texts made their way into Aquinas's hands when he was a teenager learning under Albert the Great. Partly through his meditations on the transubstantiation of the Eucharist (the conversion of sacramental bread into the flesh of Christ during the Catholic mass), Aquinas melded a central

Christian mystery with Aristotelian emphasis on natural observation and analysis, and paved the way for modern science.

To church founders like Augustine and Jerome, the mysteries of the Eucharist were best left at that. But this would not do for Aquinas. He applied reason and analysis to the metaphysical transformation of food into divine flesh and in so doing married Greek science to Judeo-Christian mysticism in what G.K. Chesterton called, though perhaps with some exaggeration, the central synthesis of Western history.[2] Moving away from the Platonism of the early Church, in which flesh was seen as a barrier of corruption between the soul and truth, Aquinas argued that it was actually *through* the windows of flesh, our senses, and not in spite of them, that we make contact with truth. In Aquinas's mind, God's incarnation into flesh as Jesus Christ clearly sanctioned the divine nature of the material world.

If Aquinas resurrected reason and analysis in Western thought, then Roger Bacon, his contemporary, established empiricism as the foundation of modern scientific thinking. Experiment was king, believed Bacon. Reason and analysis might lead us to conclusions in our observations, but only experiment could verify them. Through his own experiments, Bacon shined more light onto reality than anyone before his time. He was the first European to describe the formula for gunpowder. He wrote the first books on optics and somehow figured out that light *traveled* at some unimaginable speed (that would not be measured until the seventeenth century). After noticing that the Julian calendar had slipped by nine days, he proposed corrections that would not be officially incorporated until a few centuries later by Pope Gregory XIII. Bacon's calendar, which bears the name of the pope who sanctioned it, is the one we use today. Bacon was the earliest version of a modern scientist.[3]

What is extraordinary about Aquinas and Bacon is the *way* in which they applied their intellects. Their mode of thinking reflects the late medieval shift in the Western psyche toward, once again, left-brain values. The left hemisphere copes poorly with mystery, so it is no surprise that the central mystery of Christian life fell under Aquinas's analytical scrutiny as literacy began to intellectually re-illuminate Europe. Bacon's emphasis on the importance of experiment was not simply a personal, intellectual preference rooted in his Greco-Roman thinking: it was symptomatic of the emerging paradigm shift of the age toward the left brain and the ego.

Experiment is conducted by an ego-conscious individual. The experimenter stands apart from the experiment to objectively observe a result. The elevation of individual *experience* to chief verifier of ultimate truth tells us that the perspective of the ego was emerging once again. The pre-Socratic philosopher Protagoras, a few centuries after the alphabet rendered its ego-fueling effects onto the Greek psyche, famously said, "Man is the measure of all things." Now, in the Late Middle Ages, the individual was once again becoming the tool through which the universe measured itself.

As the Middle Ages closed, emphasis continued to shift toward the individual. Portraiture became the artistic hallmark of the coming Renaissance Period, with a focus on the *person* rather than on the archetypal hero, king, nun, or monk. We understand the achievements of Renaissance figures like Christopher Columbus, Leonardo Da Vinci, Michelangelo, and Martin Luther against the backdrop of who they were. We are just as focused, if not more so, on the *who* as on the *what* of these people. Like it or not, we find ourselves in them, be they saint or villain. Christopher Columbus, for example, is the prototype of the self-made man; a swashbuckling class-jumper with unslakable ambition.[4] This is a personality-type worshipped so intensely in the West today that its social value is an assumption seldom questioned.

As reading and writing gradually returned to Europe, the return of conscious left-brain values balanced the psychological forces of the right brain that had dominated the medieval mind. This is why we see the rise of feminism and the prominence of Mary coinciding with Greek scientific thinking during the twelfth to fourteenth centuries. We also see a shift in art toward earthy, emotive, embodied figures coupled with an emerging trend of realism expressed by Michelangelo, Donatello, Da Vinci, and later even more intensely by Caravaggio. While the right brain was calling for the rededication of human attention to the reality of body and flesh, the left brain compelled perfect, Apollonian precision of their portrayal. Consciously or unconsciously, Renaissance artists saw what Democritus saw: reality is made up of tiny particulates of matter. It is little surprise that realism became a dominant aesthetic style and portraiture a preferred mode of visual conveyance during the Renaissance.

Art did not flourish in all directions during the post-medieval period. In fact, it would come under attack especially in places like Northern Europe during the Reformation, "In the North," E.H. Gombrich tell us, "the question soon faced [artists] whether painting could or should continue at all."[5] As literacy ascended, iconoclasm arose alongside it. On his way to England in 1526 to escape the turbulence of the Reformation, the German artist Hans Holbein carried a letter of recommendation from Erasmus of Rotterdam, a Catholic priest and the original humanist. In it, Erasmus declared, "The arts here are freezing."[6] The image, so central to medieval consciousness, fell under siege as Protestant iconoclasts raged across Europe, smashing stained glass, chopping heads off statues, and stripping churches and sometimes even homes of paintings and images of any kind. Enforcing focus on the words of scripture over images,

Protestants washed the cultural landscape white. Iconoclasm was more prevalent in the Protestant north than in the Catholic south.

The revival of feminine values during the Middle Ages, exemplified by the prominence of the cult of the Virgin Mary and influential women like Hildegard, Eleanor of Aquitaine, and Joan of Arc, collapsed at the onset of the early Modern Period and remained subdued during the Reformation and Enlightenment ages. John Calvin banned women from baptizing and Martin Luther shows us in many of his writings his distrust of the opposite sex. Neither made any room for them in their new religious worldviews. It is striking when you consider that the age of universal literacy, progressive thinking, and scientific rationalism also brought with it its own degradation of human values. Europe's early Modern Period saw the revival of slavery, racism, and misogyny.

The European slave trade began in the sixteenth century, mainly to provide labor for the cash crops in the New World. The last time slaves existed on European soil was during the Greco-Roman period over a thousand years before. Rome was built on the backs of slaves, and the racism of the Greeks was well-known. They slandered the inferior languages of outsiders, generalizing their speech with the mocking sound of "bar-bar," which is how the term *barbarian* came to us. The intellectual, humanitarian, and technological accomplishments of Europe's Enlightenment Period cast a shadow of self-superiority and racism that validated the forceful penetration of its colonialism and the conceptualizing of its civilizing ideologies. Medieval Europe, on the other hand, may have been *religiously* exclusionary, yes, but race or nationalism had not been articulated in the medieval imagination. It mattered more whether you were a Christian, a Jew, or a Moor than if you were French, English, or had light or dark skin.

In classical Athens, women were wholly excluded from participating in government and married off without their say. A more extreme form of misogyny arose in Renaissance Europe as a manic European mind saw fit to burn tens of thousands of its women at the stake. As literacy spread, so did mass witch hunts, reaching their peak during the sixteenth and seventeenth centuries. Tens of thousands of women were roasted alive over fires. The reasons as to why Europe turned on its women so violently have eluded historians, but the rise of literacy was a mass-reinforcing psychological factor.[7] Slavery, witch-hunting, and imperialism marred the accomplishments of this period. It would not be until the proliferation of image-based mediums and the restoration of feminine values in the nineteenth and twentieth centuries that these ignoble positions were reversed.

The Modern Period runs from 1492 to 1945. It is the era in which humanism emerges. Humanism is the elevation of human desires, concerns, values, and problems (and a rational approach to their solutions) over and above the divine. Humanism's rise coincides with the invention of the printing press, a device that catalyzed the West's modern ego and its sense of nationalism.

CHAPTER 22:

The Rebirth of Nationhood

The very sense that [man] is united with all things is enough to sunder him from all.

~ *G.K. Chesterton*

In 1440, German goldsmith Johannes Guttenberg invented the printing press. A printing press generates letters not only faster than hand copying, but also standardizes their shapes, reinforcing a left-brained uniformity, precision, and order of which Apollo would approve. And only sixty years after the printing press was invented, a whopping twenty-million books came into print.[1]

The first books produced by the printing press were biblical translations. During the second decade of the sixteenth century, Erasmus of Rotterdam revised the original fourth-century Latin translation of the New Testament, making possible the many vernacular translations that would soon proliferate throughout Europe. A few years later, in 1522, Martin Luther used Erasmus's Latin revision to translate the New Testament into High German. The printing press made Luther's translation of the New Testament widely accessible to common Germans and fomented a unified vernacular and a broad sense of German nationalism.

Historically, nationalism is a new and bizarre phenomenon. It is a collective expression of ego-consciousness underpinned by the effects of literacy. Literacy catalyzes chronic symbolic thinking in the minds that adopt it. A nation is an abstract symbol—like the ego—held in the collective imagination of a people. It arises as a pure abstraction, like a law or an imageless God, out of the confines of the left brain. The culmination of Western nationalism during the eighteenth, nineteenth, and twentieth centuries can be traced back to the sixteenth century, when a growing sense of national consciousness began to spread in the wake of Europe's literacy revolution.

For a national consciousness to appear, Western man had to emancipate himself from three cultural legacies. The first was the "conception of temporality in which cosmology and history were indistinguishable."[2] The second was that "a particular script-language offered privileged access to ontological truth." The third legacy was "the belief that society was naturally organized around and under high centers—monarchs who were persons apart from other divine human beings and who ruled by some form of cosmological dispensation."[3] Simply put, for a nation to be possible: (1) a society needed to have a history, one separate from the natural world; (2) literacy needed to be available to the common people; and (3) rulers needed to be stripped of their divinity.

The classical Greeks emancipated themselves from the second and the third but not from the first legacy. They were unable to disentangle human history from nature, thus human history to them was subject to the unending cycle of fate and the will of the gods. The Greek mind could *scientifically* describe the contents of time within a logical, sequential, cause-and-effect framework, but time was still just cosmological and impersonal. They understood time astronomically, but they were ultimately non-historical as a society because for them the future would always repeat the past. Greek time lacked a *psychological* feature.

The Hebrews, on the other hand, met all three conditions long ago. Their society had a comparatively high literacy rate which conferred individuality on their people and prevented their kings from becoming confused with gods.[i] And, unlike the Greeks, they successfully teased their own history apart from that of the cosmos. After the creation of the universe, Israel and Yahweh strike a special contract through Avraham that focuses universal divine attention onto man and severs man's actions from the unbreakable grip of the zodiac. Man now had free will. The Hebrew conception of time was psychological. Earlier we described this cultural mindset known as "a nation" as "the corporate personality."

The European medieval mind lacked both a Judeo personal-psychological and Greco linear conception of history.[4] It did, however, have a sense of prophetic time, otherwise known as messianic time. According to messianic time, reality is the ongoing revelation of a divine plan, each of its key moments a fulfillment of something that was promised or prefigured by God. The creation of Adam is a prefiguration of the birth of Christ, for example. These two events, rather than being separated by a span of linear time, occur simultaneously. The past is immediate with the present, compressed within it, embedded in it, echoing through it.

The medieval mind felt the world in this way. Walk through any exhibit with medieval art portraying biblical episodes. Notice that the figures' clothing is always medieval. The possibility of progress, or change over time, did not occur to the medieval mind. Why then portray Jesus and his followers as wearing anything other than the garb of medieval peasants? To understand this, we must appreciate the medieval mind's feeling of time. Its sense of time corresponds to that felt by the right brain. Biblical events do not occur one after the other but instead are correlated with each other like the rhyme scheme of a song. The figure of Adam is linked to the figure of Christ; Avraham's offering of his son, Yitzhak, prefigures God's sacrifice of his son

---

[i] Though sometimes blessed or favored by Yahweh, the Hebrew kings were never divine.

Christ; the exodus of the Hebrews from Egypt corresponds to Christ's resurrection from death; and so on.

But the Greek and Judeo conceptions of time were lying dormant in the medieval psyche, ready to reemerge. And so, in what we could call the second synthesis of Judeo-Christian and Greco-Roman values, Europe alchemized a new kind of time in the late fifteenth century. This new form of time is psycho-spatial and produces the effect of national consciousness.

Walter Benjamin called this new time *homogenous, empty time.*[5] It is *homogenous* in that each part of it (seconds, minutes, days, weeks, months) is equivalent (that is, all seconds are the same, all minutes are the same, etc.). The new time is *empty* in that each part of it is spatial: multiple events and actions can coincide simultaneously *within* the frame of a minute or an hour or a day. Homogenous, empty time is Greek in that it is uniform, objective, and spatial; events happen inside of it. It can be measured by a clock or calendar. But spatial time by itself cannot produce national consciousness. There must be a psychological component. That component was the corporate personality. To the Hebrews, time *was* event, it did not *contain* events. Events do not occur *in* time, the events *are* time. *Event* is action, which is the very nature of reality itself. The corollary of the omnitemporal God (the only being capable of experiencing the entire event or image of reality all at once) was Israel. The Hebrews conceived themselves as Israel in this light. Thanks to this worldview, each Israelite felt themselves in personal relationship with God and he to them. Each Israelite could feel contemporaneous with all past, present, and future members of their tribe.

Without this personal, individualized feature of the national image, there is no real national future, no innovation, no progress, no change, no true possibility of something different. For the Hebrews, their collective moral *choices*, their actions, as the prophets warned so many times, determined Israel's future, which was ultimately a function of their having heeded, or not heeded, God's laws. Without a *real* future—one that is influenced by our choices—the individual and indeed the nation are nothing more than unconscious automatons. The ideas of change, progress, and hope for a better future come out of this sensibility. And they are largely unexamined assumptions of Western progressive thinking.

A person aware of psycho-spatial time can feel themselves contemporaneous at one moment with a horde of anonymous people connected by a shared set of ideas, language, values, and politics. Within psycho-spatial time, I can be aware that as I type these words, my neighbor is making dinner while a colleague of mine in Texas is watching TV. These events happen simultaneously, and though I can conceive them abstractly, I do not perceive them concretely.

Melded together, Greek spatial and Judeo psychological time produce the effect of national consciousness because they combine the Greek temporal structure of cause and effect and a Hebrew psychological God-view of events. While linear cause and effect allows us to feel our past as a chain of causality, the corporate personality acts as historical lifeblood flowing through causality, giving us a sense of personal and collective (national, racial, ideological) contemporaneity with other people. This is our living, modern consciousness. In fact, this God-view perspective of events provides the perspective necessary for a novel, a literary phenomenon that coincided with the appearance of nationalism.[6] This is why the West's first novel was written in the early eighteenth century.

The novel makes the reader aware of the simultaneous action of different people in disparate situations, people who are or can be anonymous to each other. The author takes on an omniscient God-view. From the perspective of nationalism, this allows a person to become conscious of a simultaneity across a community of people moving lockstep in a forward flow of succession in accordance with the increments of a calendar. A Norwegian or Romanian, though anonymous to millions of fellow Norwegians or Romanians, and he to them, can imagine his actions as simultaneous with theirs at any moment and feel contemporaneous with them, as well as with a timeless Norwegian-ness or Romanian-ness.

The epicenter of modern consciousness shares the same ground as the great fracture of the Church into Protestant and Catholic: that is, sixteenth-century Germany. This is the same region in which the printing press was invented. Martin Luther, the de facto leader of the Reformation, introduced a new kind of individualism into the West.

Because Luther believed that the words of the scripture itself, and not the clergy, carried true authority, it must be up to the *individual* (reading text in solitude) to mediate their own relationship with God. That relationship was to be through one's own person, not through the corrupt Catholic clergy, who had discredited themselves and profaned their office by selling indulgences to finance extravagant dinners, parties, and papal tombs. "Every man is his own priest," Luther said.

Luther was a man who, at a time when executions of heretics were not at all uncommon, openly defied ecclesiastical authority because of his *conscience*. After being summoned to the city of Worms to recant his works, including those that criticized the powers of the Church and the ones that did not, Luther refused, saying: "I cannot and I will not retract anything, for it is neither safe nor right to go against conscience."[7]

Cahill asks, "Was there ever a figure in history more attached to his subjective identity—to his "I"—than Martin Luther?"[8] He continues:

> "Nowhere in our earlier history does the force of ego ring so fully and defiantly as in the scene at Worms, where Brother Martin—this 'pile of shit,' as he so

> often called himself—dared to say no to the assembled forces of early modern Europe, to the entire panoply of church and state, and to cite his own little conscience (surely a negligible phenomenon to the majority of his listeners) as the reason for his absolute, unnuanced, unhedged rebellion."[9]

Was Luther's conscience, this unignorable inner voice, the same Voice that spoke to Avraham at Harran? Was this part of the same inner phenomenon that compelled Avraham to depart Harran on a seeming suicide mission into the desert "to the land that I will let you see?" Was it the same source of conflict within Augustine? We are asked by Cahill to "pause before this figure of Martin Luther and acknowledge both his astonishing contemporaneity and our, perhaps somewhat uncomfortable, brotherhood with him."[10]

Could the Voice that compelled Avraham and Luther to go out and do the unheard of, be the same one that dialogues with us inside our skulls every day? Is this the voice that we, in the modern secular age of near-universal literacy, take for granted? Without alphabetic literacy, it is unlikely that our psyches could organize into a single voice so intensely as to become a unified stream of consciousness speaking back to us in our heads. Surely the nature of our self-talk—its tone, attitude, and mood—is shaped by our culture and upbringing, but the fact that there is a voice to dialogue with in the first place is an easily overlooked miracle of self-consciousness. When we consider Avraham and the Patriarchs, Pythagoras, Plato, Alexander the Great, Christ, Augustine, Aquinas, and Luther in this light, we can peer down the line of our psychological inheritance and see the historical unfolding of the sacred experience of being aware of awareness. And with its light must come its shadow.

CHAPTER 23:

Faust, Modern Man's Myth

We are living in a culture entirely hypnotized by the illusion of time, in which the so-called present moment is felt as nothing but an infinitesimal hairline between an all-powerfully causative past and an absorbingly important future. We have no present. Our consciousness is almost completely preoccupied with memory and expectation. We do not realize that there never was, is, nor will be any other experience other than present experience.

~ Alan Watts

If there is one quintessential myth of modernity, one that encapsulates modern man's dilemma of self-consciousness, it is the legend of Faust. And like all legends, its many retellings welded its central character to myth, enshrouding the person of Faust in mystery. Some question the very existence of Faust, while others claim the actual person was a fifteenth-century partner and creditor of Johannes Guttenberg named Johann Faust.

Eighteen years after Martin Luther finished his translation of the New Testament, an alchemist by the name of Johann Georg Faust was killed in an explosion in a German border town. Before his untimely end, Faust traveled from town to town performing horoscopes, necromancy, magic, and he even worked as a physician.

Faust's story has held the attention of the West ever since. A few decades after his death, the first chapbook about his life appeared. Published by Johann Spies in 1587, *Historia von D Johann Fausten* circulated throughout Germany before catching the attention of Christopher Marlowe, the English playwright and contemporary of Shakespeare, who used it as the basis of his famous play *The Tragical History of Doctor Faustus*. Since Marlowe's version, an estimated twenty-thousand books have been written about the legend, the most famous of these being the 1832 play by Johann Von Goethe, called *Faust*.[1] Published one year after Goethe's death, it is one of the most often-quoted works of literature.

The essential legend is, like all myths that characterize their eras, familiar both individually and collectively, both consciously and unconsciously: the main character sells his soul to the devil in exchange for worldly knowledge and power. This is the archetypal temptation of modern man.

According to the original sixteenth-century tale, Faust makes a twenty-four-year contract with the devil named Mephistopheles. Faust's worldly exploits, from scholarly pursuits to love to political power, are enabled and maximized by Mephistopheles. Each exploit comes at a price felt by those around Faust. These range, in Goethe's version, from Faust's impregnation of Gretchen and her subsequent disgrace to the destruction of Philemon and Baucis' countryside cottage.

The myth was originally a cautionary tale about the lures of the world—power, sex, fame, and money—displacing man's original goal of eternal salvation with God. Its writing was intertwined with the contemporary politics of the great schism of the Catholic Church. Spies' *Historia*, for example, was written expressly for the purpose of warning fellow Protestants from straying from the Christian path Luther had outlined.

But like all cautionary tales that ostensibly forbid this or that, as a rule they incite more interest in whatever it is they burn, ban, or censor. Their secret purpose, it seems then, is to realize and encourage the antithetical path. Relying on man's *yetzer hara,* God forbade the fruit of the Tree of Knowledge of Good and Evil *just so that* Adam would eat it.[i] Faust embodies the pinnacle desires of man's wayward spirit in the modern age, seeking to know the secrets of nature, dominating the Earth through force of will and intellect, storming the gates of Heaven, throwing down its ruler and usurping the throne.

One of Faust's primary pursuits is supreme knowledge. This represents the conflict between Western man's medieval and modern worldviews, the former characterized by faith, the latter by knowledge. Faust restlessly pursues exhaustive knowledge of the world and of himself. Mystery is unacceptable. Mephistopheles asks Faust: "Have you not, with bold impudence, defined—and in the most forceful language, too—God, and the world, and all that moves therein, and what goes on in human minds and hearts?"[2]

Whereas the original renditions of the Faust myth are simplistic in their moral parsing of the world into good and evil, Protestant and Catholic, and so on, Goethe's *Faust* introduces two dramatic innovations that end up making over the core legend and complicating the character of Faust.[3] First, Goethe replaces the contract between Faust and Mephistopheles with a wager. Second, Goethe reverses Faust's ultimate fate. He grants Faust, despite the destruction and suffering he is responsible for, escape from Mephistopheles' clutches in his final moment and has him carried off to Heaven instead of to Hell. Both changes thrust Faust as well as our attention into the present moment.

Cahill reminds us that the only kind of *real* future is one we do not know. Faust's wager produces this real future because,

---

[i] The breath of life conferred by Yahweh into Adam contained both the *yetzer hatov* (inclination for good) and the *yetzer hara* (inclination for evil or selfish desire or *wayward spirit*). This being implanted in him from the very first, man was "set up" by God from the beginning to stray. This was, of course, ultimately necessary so that God could come to know himself through man.

unlike a contract, the outcome of a wager is not set. Faust's end is no longer preset: it could go either way. On the other hand, a contract, like the fate of the ancients, seals Faust's future from the beginning. Ancient man saw the universe as an ever-repeating cycle that, like the seasons and the stars, rotated in a circle forever. There was no real future, just a replay of what came before. There was, accordingly, no real individual to speak of, no *free* experience (in the sense in which we moderns mean it). The historical appearance of the ego can only occur under conditions in which the future has become a reality. And only under these conditions do we become free. Because we do not know and do not control the future, "we are not doomed, not bound to some predetermined fate; we are free. If anything can happen," Cahill declares, "we are truly liberated."[4]

And free will only becomes possible under conditions of limitation. If we are bound up with the infinite, the ever-repeating cycle of eternity, then there can be no individual separate from an external world, because in this model there is no division between the external and internal worlds. Here, the individual is undifferentiated from *the* continuous event of the universe that we call Now, a great seamless, simultaneous happening. The fundamental psychological project of the individual, then, is cutting the eternal Now into a past, present, and future. The tension between eternity and time is central to Faust's consciousness.

According to the wager between Mephistopheles and Faust, Mephistopheles is awarded Faust's soul only *if* Mephistopheles, by enabling Faust's worldly undertakings, delivers Faust into a moment of true satisfaction, which is to say into the Now:

If on a bed of sloth I ever lie contented,
may I be done for then and there!
If ever you, with lies and flattery,

can lull me into self-complacency
or dupe me with a life of pleasure,
may that day be the last for me!
This is my wager!

If I should ever say to any moment:
Tarry, remain!—you are so fair!
Then you may lay your fetters on me,
then I will gladly be destroyed!...
...the clock may stop, its hand may fall,
and time at last for me be over![5]

Faust forfeits his soul if he surrenders to the bliss of the present. It is not difficult to see in the excerpt above that while Faust relies on his inability to commit himself to the moment (thus winning the wager), he yearns to surrender to its felt immediacy. Ironically, the insistence of the future becomes a dominant subtext of the myth.[6] Faust represents you and me, the modern person who cannot face the Absolute experience of the present and instead must take up psychic residence in the past or the future, always *streben* (striving) for that elusive state of arrival. "It is to strive with all my might that I am promising to do."[7]

Tortured by the prospect of a better future, modern man is seldom comfortable in the Now, which is to say, seldom comfortable with himself. Like Faust, he is never satisfied. There is no final goal to his pursuits, no point of rest and fulfillment.

For Faust, "pursuit itself," David Wellberry explains, "regardless of its goal, is primary."[8] Faust's reality is a constant anticipation of more, each achievement a staging point for the next. The manic pace at which modern humanity pursues progress, improvement of the world, and improvement of itself is a *Faustian* state of consciousness. And in a *Faustian* state, the Infinite and the mystical realms of experience are unavailable:

"The Great Spirit rejected me with scorn, and Nature's doors are closed against me."[9]

Nature's doors are like Dostoevsky's[ii] stone wall that his Underground Man bumps up against:

> "Impossibility—meaning a stone wall? What stone wall? Well, of course, the laws of nature, the conclusions of natural science, mathematics. Once it's proved to you that you descended from an ape, there's no use making a wry face, just take it for what it is... go ahead and accept it, there's nothing to be done, because two times two is—mathematics. Try objecting to that."[10]

The Underground Man is objecting to the same frustration that plagues Faust: finitude. It is felt as the stone wall of limitation, a limit imposed on man by his very own objectification of the world through scientific rationalism and the ego-reinforcing effects of literacy. Faust's compulsive striving is a blatant denial of his mortality, a rejection of his finitude. The present moment is relativized or missed, and death put off by focusing on the next thing to achieve, gain, conquer, improve, destroy, or consume.

For this reason, Faust enlists Mephistopheles to assist him in doubling down on the phenomenal world of linear time. Faust throws himself into experience and the oscillation between gain and loss that comes with it:

> "Let us sate the fervors of passion in depths of
> sensuality!

[ii] Dostoevsky was ten-years-old when Goethe died.

> Let's plunge into the torrents of time, in the
> whirl of eventful existence."[11]

If we could momentarily set aside our must-dos, deadlines, goals, distractions, our longing for the things that once were, our anticipation of things that may or may not ever be, the people we once had or could have, we would find ourselves face-to-face with the epicenter of creation, the abyss of Now. And it is only in the Now that the symbol of me, my ego, dissolves; an experience metaphysically synonymous—at least to an ego—with obliteration, death, and perhaps even Hell.

And although ostensibly Mephistopheles' end of the bet is to bring Faust into this ultimate moment of supreme euphoria and final satisfaction, his real intention is concealed by a brilliant deception. So long as he can keep Faust's eye steadily on the future, his feet cycling the hamster wheel of ever more, all under the pretext of working to attain the opposite, Mephistopheles achieves his end. His real goal is to endlessly enable Faust's future, not bring him to an end moment of rest to which Faust can finally say, "Tarry, remain!—you are so fair!" Mephistopheles already has Faust's soul. The wager was won for Mephistopheles before it began.

Mephistopheles symbolizes the ego. He is the Deceiver, the personification of the great mistake, the original sin, of the human mind in confusing its real identity with a self that it articulates out of its past and future. The faster Faust chases his moment of bliss, the faster it runs away. In the same way, the ego tries to satiate its desire by chasing a vision of a future that, even if realized in the world, somehow never quite satisfies, and so the interminable chase goes on. We are reminded of the parched and famished Tantalus, doomed in tortured frustration to grasp at food and water that recede just out of his reach until the end of time.[iii] This is the great deception of Mephistopheles and the great deception of ego-consciousness. For the ego resides not in the living world of the moment, but in the dead world of memory and the not-yet world of anticipation.

Faust's paradoxical yearning for the moment and his inability to surrender to it discloses modern man's total alienation from the world. This plays out in Faust's final act of will in his encounter with Philemon and Baucis.

Philemon and Baucis are the Phrygian couple from Greco-Roman mythology who provide hospitality and food to two weary sojourners who, after being properly welcomed by the old couple, reveal themselves as Zeus and Hermes (or Jupiter and Mercury). All of the other people in Eumeneia refused hospitality to Zeus and Hermes. As reward, the elderly pair are granted any wish they desire. They wish for their home to be made into a temple with them as its stewards and to be taken by death at the same moment so that neither has to live in the world without the other. Both wishes are granted. After the meal, Zeus commands Philemon and Baucis to climb a hill for high ground, insisting that they are not to look back as he floods their hometown and kills its inhabitants as punishment for violating the ancient code of hospitality. As the couple finally reach the top of the hill, breathless and soaked by rain, they affirm their love for each other through tears and turn back just in time to see Eumeneia sink beneath the waves before Philemon is turned into an oak tree and Baucis into a linden. And there the pair of trees stand for centuries—symbols of love and strength—as sentinels overlooking the temple below.

Goethe inserts his own version of this legend into the fifth and final act of his play. By this point, Faust has come to own all the land in the region except for the quaint piece of real estate lived on by the legendary couple. He covets their land, but they

---

[iii] This is from where we get the word *tantalize*.

refuse to give it up. He sends Mephistopheles to evict them with an offer of a better piece of land somewhere else. But instead of making a deal, Mephistopheles and his henchmen kill the couple and a guest of theirs and burn down their cottage and its little chapel. This final act of Faust makes us face the darkest place of our own hearts.

The legend of Philemon and Baucis symbolizes the sacredness of hospitality, of bringing respite to a stranger—and provides a warning of the destructive consequences of doing the opposite. The point is that man, like Zeus and Hermes, is a wayfarer in a world that in the end should reveal itself as his home. The gods' act of transforming the couple's house into a temple for their act of hospitality ratifies the sacredness of the world as man's home. This is in contrast to the inhospitable and profane world confronted by Zeus and Hermes during their tour of Eumeneia before their encounter with Philemon and Baucis. By welcoming the strangers as guests, Philemon and Baucis reveal the true nature of the world to man. In turn, the strangers reveal their true nature to Philemon and Baucis. Joined together at the table, man and the divine break bread.

This mutual revelation between God and man symbolizes the process of man's own self-revelation: he has in the first half of life tricked himself into feeling a stranger in the world (alienated from the world from the perspective of his ego), but in life's second phase, he must unmask himself so that he remembers the world as his source, both his beginning and end. Zeus's command to the couple to not look back as they climb to safety, points at the fact that the past, which lies behind us, is inaccessible. And when we dare look back upon it, we turn rigid and dead.[iv]

[iv] In Genesis, Lot and his wife were told to not look back as they retreated from Sodom, the famous biblical city destroyed with hellfire by God because it, too, failed to observe the laws of hospitality. When Lot's wife turns to look back at Sodom, she is turned, not into a linden like Baucis, but into a pillar of salt.

The ego arises by living in the past and objectifying the world, which is to say that the existence of ego requires at a minimum a level of alienation from reality. And yet even at its worst throughout history, man's distance from the world was always soothed by some unforgettable reminder of his unseverable connection to it (through ritual, myth, mystical experience, and so forth). But now this alienation reaches its event horizon in the modern Faust and perhaps in us as well. Goethe turns the ending of Philemon and Baucis tragic. Philemon and Baucis are stripped of their opportunity to provide man the antidote to his alienation.

By destroying the old couple's home, razing the chapel, and killing their guest—a lone wanderer, who may be Jehovah or even Faust himself in a parallel dimension—Faust cements man's total alienation from the world. In Philemon and Baucis' home, at the meal they shared with their guests, "There it was. That gift of the eternal moment," Wellberry says, "The gift of the world. The chance to be truly Faustus the fortunate, the happy one sitting here with this elderly, generous couple. And it cannot be received."[12]

Instead, Faust has burned down his home in the world and killed his gods. Faust's final act precludes man's redemptive act of self-revelation. Man finds himself an irredeemable wayfarer, forever lost, a permanent stranger in his own house who clings to his ego out of fear of the abyss he senses beyond. "Like Oedipus before him," Wellberry continues, "Faust is rendered at the play's end blind. He cannot see the world and the world's gift. Modernity, in its mono obsession—Faust's tragic end tells us—incinerates the house of hospitality, sets the richest of all gifts, the gift of the present moment, into flames."[13]

No longer is the world the Great Mother, a place where man may rest his weary soul for a time. The Great Mother of nature is enemy, or dead and mute. Now the world is a nightmare man woke up to, a place that, due to its sheer otherness and knack for getting in the way of man's ego-desires, must be subdued, perfected, and eventually destroyed.

Having witnessed firsthand the Napoleonic wars that tore through Europe during the second half of his life, Goethe must have sensed this impulse of suicidal mania rising up inside of man. Goethe's anxiety anticipated two global wars; a genocide against the people who conferred their God to the West; and the invention of man's ultimate suicide weapon, the atom bomb, some hundred years after Goethe's death.

The legend of Faust signals the historical moment in which the psyche of the European West began to emerge out of its medieval worldview. The sharp ascendancy of ego-consciousness, a further fall out of nature into Luther's self-described pile-of-shitness, temporally coincided with the cracking of the foundation of the Judeo-Christian myth.

Faust is about the modern individual and the interaction of its growing rational, intellectual, and objectifying energies with the world. Its conception as a myth serves as commentary on the West's imperialism, its nihilism, its capitalistic enterprising, its scientific revolutions, its mastery over and rampant exploitation of nature, its invention of mass production and gluttonous overconsumption of material objects. It signals Western man's increasing powers of mental abstraction and insistence on the future by circumventing the concrete constraints of the present—or at least staving off its immediate demands—through financial magic such as fractional-reserve banking and paper currency (which Faust and Mephistopheles invent in Part II of the play). The legend of Faust points at the West's revival of democracy and the sanctification of its most precious component, the individual, as the center of the universe. As the projection of the God-image tumbled out of the sky over the course of the eighteenth and nineteenth centuries, man's ego filled the vacuum. The cosmos opened up onto infinity, chased by man's hunger for absolute understanding, power, and immortality.

CHAPTER 24:

Modernity: Discovering the Unconscious

Unless we prefer to be made fools of by our illusions, we shall, by carefully analyzing every fascination, extract from it a portion of our own personality, like a quintessence, and slowly come to recognize that we meet ourselves time and again in a thousand disguises on the path of life.

~ *C.G. Jung*[1]

Faust was a literary product of the left-brained paternalism that had overtaken Europe in its Reformation and Enlightenment periods. But even toward the end of Goethe's life, the pendulum of consciousness was swinging back toward feminine values. The invention of image mediums like the photograph (1826), the kinetoscope (1891) and the television (1926) helped revive unconscious, right-brain perspectives. Michael Faraday's conceptualization of *the field* (1846)—a pervasive, energy-propagating medium through which forces like electromagnetism and gravity are transmitted—also contributed to the revival of the right-brain worldview. The yin of the psyche, the unconscious, was first identified and studied during the nineteenth century.

The most revolutionary effect, and in turn magnifying factor, of the modern paradigm shift was the invention of the internet (1983). Both the function and effects of the internet are feminine in nature. It connects, in no hierarchy or order, the distributed contents of the world-wide web. Shlain points out that "both the internet and the world-wide web are not linear; they are holistic. All ancient deities associated with webs and nets were goddesses."[2]

Internet social media has intensified the resurgence of the image and deemphasized the written word. Throughout almost all social media applications, the conventions of grammar are loosened and informalized into cyber slang. Many social media platforms today stream hundreds or even thousands of images a day into the eyes of over a billion iPhone users. There are at least four-billion smartphone owners on the planet.[3] Perceptive tendencies of the right brain (such as connection, harmony, holism, intuition, and feeling) have been resurrected and poured into the collective psychological smelter along with modernity's left-brain, masculine values (and its perceptive biases) of separation, hierarchy, order, analysis, and thinking. This recollection—the recall of the Goddess, collectivism, nature, chaos, feminism, irrationalism, eternity, the unconscious psyche, and tribalism—has reshaped the landscapes of modern art, music, religion, politics, and science.

Some thirty years before Goethe's masterwork was published, the holistic thinking of the East had already begun to penetrate the West. In 1801, Anquetil du Perron catalyzed the revival of Western occultism by publishing a translation of fifty *Upanishads* he procured from India in the late 1700s. Following this influx of Eastern thought, Helena Blavatsky and Rudolf Steiner attempted to synthesize natural science and religion in their theological projects of Theosophy and Anthroposophy, respectively. Transcendentalist Ralph Waldo Emerson expressed the deep, invisible unity of humanity in his essay, "The Over-Soul" (1841), and encouraged people to return to nature to reconnect with their intuition.

The West's sense of humanness began to change. It became apparent in the nineteenth century that humans were neither the first beings to appear on the planet nor biologically exceptional across its myriad forms. It came to be understood that some cultures had progressed to sophisticated states of civilization and consciousness while others were still living out an older, primitive, and unconscious way of life. As limiting and damaging as this viewpoint proved to be, it was nonetheless a sign that the West was now becoming aware of humanity's *unconscious* or prehistoric past. Prehistory is to history what non-reflection is to self-reflection. The West was still recovering from Columbus's startling discovery of the primitive tribes dwelling in the Eden of the Americas. After stumbling upon what must have looked like humanity in its childhood, the West began looking farther back into time.

It is not coincidence that at the same time the West became aware of the unconscious, it shined a flashlight into the past before recorded time (that is, *conscious* time). The axiom of the origin of man as the descendants of Adam and Eve was obsolete.[i] *Prehistory* became a formal subject of study during the nineteenth century. The field of archeology emerged. Sir Arthur Evans (1851–1941) discovered and excavated Minoan Crete, Europe's first civilization. Flinders Petrie (1853–1942) excavated Egyptian ruins and in so doing laid the methodological foundation of the study of prehistoric, megalithic sites as well as future Egyptology. The beginning of existence was pushed back from thousands to millions and then billions of years when Arthur Holmes (1890–1960) in 1912 dated a specimen of rock to an age of 1.6-billion years.

---

[i] It should be noted that the myth of Eden was never meant to be conceived as history. Dogmatization of the myth as historical fact of human origination by the likes of James Ussher (circa seventeenth century) and others, sucked life and meaning out of the myth.

Speculations on the role of government were recast through a right-brain lens. After living in a cabin near Walden Pond (and a brief stint in jail), Henry David Thoreau wrote "Civil Disobedience" in 1849, declaring "that government is best which governs not at all," reflecting on the apolitical and anarchical modalities of natural, prehistoric man. A year earlier, Karl Marx published the *Communist Manifesto* in which he and Friedrich Engels conceptualized a world workers' revolution as an inevitable outcome to human history and a reaction to the oppressive nature of capitalism. Core communist principles of shared property and collectivism correspond to the imagined egalitarian economics of prehistoric man. In 1864, Fyodor Dostoyevsky published *Notes from Underground,* exposing the irrational and paradoxical nature of man's underground or *unconscious* psyche as a warning to his politically zealous contemporaries about the dangers of forcing societies into theorized utopias. Drowning out the death rattle of absolute monarchy with louder calls for democracy and *laissez-faire* markets, capitalists themselves were shifting away from left-brained paternalism.

The most recognizable symbol of fascism, the swastika, is actually a primordial, prehistoric gestalt that represents the original unity of the cosmos and the Self. It is the basis of many old religious symbols, including the cross and the mandala. It comes from the Sanskrit word *svastika,* which means "well-being." The Nazi ideologues co-opted the image to link their ethno-racial purity movement to the prehistoric Aryan (Indo-European) peoples. Prehistoric values (like egalitarianism, communal consciousness, and tribalism) were revivified in different ways through the sociopolitical structures of capitalism, socialism, fascism, and communism.

Assumptions about human rights, gender relationships, and sex dissolved and then reformed in a bath of egalitarian ideals of prehistoric partnership. Slavery was widely abolished during the nineteenth century. In the first half of the twentieth century, widespread women's suffrage was achieved, colonialism collapsed, and major feminist movements emerged. During the second half of the twentieth century, two more feminist movements surfaced, the green movement appeared and successfully lobbied environmental-friendly policy into legislature, and in 1964 the Civil Rights Act was signed into US law. Toward the end of the twentieth century, Black feminist Kimberle Williams Crenshaw, in an attempt to expose the comprehensiveness of institutionalized oppression, argued that the oppression of women intersected with social and political discrimination. The #blacklivesmatter and #metoo movements are recent memes of these positions. Celebration of pride, diversity, and open sexuality by the LGBTQ community blurs gender and sex categories, drawing on an admittedly naïve reimagination of a prehistoric era in which human beings lived in cultural anarchy.

The discovery of the unconscious occurred when man's soul fell under the crosshairs of human intellectual control. Over the course of human history, we can trace the focal point of humanity's divine projection from the animals of the Paleolithic to the plants of the Neolithic, to the heavens of the Bronze Age, and finally to man himself in the modern age.[4] Each phase occupied human attention and wonder until each subject was brought under social and intellectual control. Paleolithic cave paintings identified man in combination with the dangerous animals he hunted (and was sometimes hunted by). But the domestication of animals during the great agricultural revolution would bring this to an end. With the dawn of animal husbandry, the divine projection shifted to plants. We then see the cycles of planting and harvesting identified with human procreation within the fertility cults of the Neolithic Period. Once the cycles of growing were inculcated into man's psyche, we turned our attention to the skies, built ziggurats, and discovered celestial gods and the endless pattern of the spheres. Astrology attempted to link these patterns to human destiny.

It would not be until the Ptolemaic and then Copernican models of astronomy brought the celestial mysteries under intellectual control that man finally turned the object of wonder inward to himself. Unchained from the fates, the never-ending spinning of the celestial bodies above, man became a free, ethically responsible being. Shakespeare recognized this when he has Cassius say: "The fault, dear Brutus is not in our stars, but in ourselves."

When Western man finally became self-aware enough to peer inward, he discovered the unconscious. During the nineteenth century the unconscious would undergo analysis by a new kind of science called psychology. By applying psychoanalysis to his patients' dreams, Sigmund Freud shocked prudish Victorians with the revelation that their egos were holding at bay the uncivilized instincts of their primal past. Freud thought that the psyche was made up of three parts: the id, the ego, and the superego. The id blindly pursues gratification of primal urges like eating, drinking, eliminating, fighting, and sex; the superego represses these desires according to cultural mores; while the ego balances the two opposing forces into relationship. An admirer and student of Freud, Carl Jung conceived the *collective* unconscious based on his predecessor's model. Unlike Freud who limited the scope of the unconscious to an individual person, Jung saw it also as a collective container of all of the knowledge, experiences, and memories of the human species across time.

One of the first late modern persons to make conscious contact with the unconscious was Friedrich Nietzsche. As a classicist, Nietzsche was disturbed by how much Enlightenment thinkers had attributed classical Greek culture to the fulfillment of the energies of Apollo. Greece was not the culmination of the energies that produced its reasonable, stoic, white sculptures, he thought. Nietzsche believed that it was, in fact, the cults of dark Dionysus and their music that lay at the foundation of the creativity, purpose, aspirations, and grandeur of the Greek mind—and hence the Western mind.[5] In *Twilight of the Idols,* Nietzsche exclaims, "And with that I again touch on my earliest point of departure: *The Birth of Tragedy* was my first revaluation of all values. And on that point I again stand on the earth out of which my intention, my ability grows—I, the last disciple of the philosopher Dionysus—I, the teacher of the eternal recurrence."[6]

Nietzsche had no patience for those in his time who eschewed life, "ye despisers of the body." These are the people we know today who see human life on Earth as a corrupt aberration within a meaningless cosmos, "Therefore are ye now angry with life and with the Earth. And unconscious envy is in the sidelong look of your contempt."[7] These are also the ones who, after having some level of tragedy visit them, find life ultimately empty, miserable, and out to get them. For them, life is drudgery. But for Nietzsche, it was only from the standpoint of a tragic worldview that we can we begin to affirm life. We could not know its joy, gains, and successes unless we also accepted its complementary experiences of misery, loss, and failures. This is why we must, as Nietzsche exclaimed, say "yes to life even in its strangest and most painful episodes."[8]

Summing it up in his famous declaration *God is Dead!* Nietzsche understood that the dissolution of the Judeo-Christian myth by reason, science, materialism, and technology posed psychological risks to modern man. Nietzsche understood that good and evil were no longer predefined absolutes but relative—what is good for the lion is bad for the sheep, and vice versa. Modern man, like the Greeks in the face of their crisis, had to channel Dionysian energies to reform a value structure within a now meaningless and infinite cosmos. The God-image had fallen out of Heaven into man.

What is man? Where did he come from? Where is he going? Without the Judeo-Christian myth to supply answers to these questions, new answers had to be found. To Nietzsche, this presented man with an opportunity to "create beyond himself." In other words, man was poised for greatness, for a leap to what he called the superman. "Dead are all the gods," says Nietzsche through the mouth of the prophet Zarathustra. "Now do we desire the superman to live."[9] To Nietzsche, the superman was man reborn, man transformed beyond himself, a teleology twisted by the Nazi movement into a eugenic ideology.[ii]

Goethe, Dostoevsky, and Nietzsche realized that without meaning supplied by the afterlife promises of the Christian myth, the pain of existence could no longer be justified. No salvation was awaiting man at the end of his life, just a black void of nonexistence. What was the point of life, then? Without meaning, there can be no redemption to our suffering. Perhaps humanity would be better off eradicating pain from the world and maximizing pleasure. Humanity seemed destined to turn to the state to compensate for the loss of salvation after death. If Heaven was not available after death, we must bring it to Earth in this life.

In exchange for the collective power of its individuals, the state would promise to provide such conditions. The expansion of the power of the state could only come at the expense of the power (and the reality) of the individual. In other words, the individual, unable to bear the pain of existence, surrenders the Self back to the state in a great, historical reversal. The ethos of Stalinism, Maoism and modern North Korea embody the consequences of this reversal. But this psychological defeat plays out on some level in the capitalistic West, too, where the individual existentially medicates itself through endless

[ii] Some of Nietzsche's writings were corrupted by his anti-Semitic sister Elizabeth Forster-Nietzsche, who became the steward of her brother's works at the end of his life.

material distraction, amusement, and consumption, all the way to the grave.

Goethe and Dostoevsky smelled the utopias coming.[iii] Nietzsche feared that Western man would become emasculated and that the sovereign individual, something the West had worked so hard to build, would die a painful death. Dionysus, Nietzsche recognized, was desperately needed again.

[iii] See Fyodor Dostoevsky's *Notes from Underground* (New York: Vintage Books, 1993).

CHAPTER 25:

Dionysus: Antidote for Ego-Consciousness

At his conception the earthly was touched by the splendor of divine Heaven. But in this union of the heavenly with the earthly...man's tear-filled lot was not dissolved but preserved, rather, in sharp contrast to superhuman majesty. He who was born in this way is not only the exultant god, the god who brings man joy. He is the suffering and dying god, the god of tragic contrast. And the inner force of this dual reality is so great that he appears among men like a storm, he staggers them, and he tames their opposition with the whip of madness. All tradition, all order must be shattered. Life becomes suddenly an ecstasy—an ecstasy of blessedness, but an ecstasy, no less, of terror.

~ Walter Otto[1]

The Greek mind in its classical period faced an existential crisis like that faced by the West today. After the alphabet took hold in Greece, ego-consciousness ascended; the old gods of ancient Mycenae receded into the background; and the energies of rationalism, order, individuality, and boundaries swept the culture. Can we summon a more supreme image of the individual than Greece's perfectly sculpted statues of the human figure poised grandly atop Athenian marble? Apollo himself was the sculptor god, and through him Greek artists freed the human form from undifferentiated blocks of matter, like birthing creation out of chaos. Dionysus, on the other hand, was the remedial pressure-release to a culture rendered painfully ego-conscious by the alphabet. Whereas Apollo is the "embodiment of limitation...with Dionysus comes the collapse of individuality and restraint. Apollo sculpts the self, Dionysus wreaks its destruction, redeeming man from the ego."[2]

Dionysus is the mythological embodiment of the unconscious. He is the dark lord of ancient Greece. Effeminate, with flowing dark hair, sometimes androgynous in appearance, a god of ecstasy and madness, he is the yin, surrounded by nymphs and satyrs—the goat-footed, horned, bearded man-creatures sporting pulsing erections, whose image became the pagan god Pan and the devil.[i]

Dionysus is regularly contrasted with his opposite, the sun god Apollo—lord of light, order, truth, and justice, whose arrow never misses its mark. Apollo represents the left-brain values of order and rationalism, while Dionysus represents the right-brain values of chaos and feeling. Apollo slayed Python, the dragon-guard of the sea. Dionysus is the other who brings madness, always coming from beyond the pale.

> "The Madness which is called Dionysus is no sickness, no debility in life, but a companion of life at its healthiest. It is the tumult which erupts from its innermost recesses when they mature and force their way to the surface. It is the madness inherent in the womb of the mother. It attends all moments of creation, instantly changes ordered existence into chaos, and ushers in primal salvation and primal pain and, in both, the primal wildness of being."[3]

[i] This association was made later by the Christians.

Conjoined together, Apollo and Dionysus produced the creative tension from which the richness of Greek culture sprang. And it was from the domain of Dionysus—this "earth" as Nietzsche called it, this ground of the unconscious—that Nietzsche stood as the last disciple of the dark lord, encouraging the tragic/ecstatic disposition toward life in a dawning post-modern age.

The tragic/ecstatic disposition embraces the paradoxical nature of reality. As Heraclitus understood that reality was in flux, a constant collision of opposites, and as Pythagoras realized that existence sprang into being by the application of duality onto unity, in the same way does Dionysus stand beyond the opposites as the ambivalent god, witness to their song. From his perspective, reality is a marriage of good and evil, life and death, anguish and ecstasy, love and hate, elation and depression, loss and gain, suffering and bliss. The one cannot be experienced and understood without experiencing and understanding its opposite.

Central to the tragic plays of Dionysian spring festivals in classical Greece were the satiric choruses. Acting was *not* the essential component of the plays (and may not even have been a part of the very first Greek dramas). The music of the choruses was paramount. The choruses were made up of Dionysian satyrs who sung in satyr-ic[ii] fashion. It is interesting to think about what the satiric song may have sounded like. Plato and Aristotle called the sound *dithyramb*, which means "wild oration." A spontaneously directed primordial chant is no less than a direct expression of the unconscious itself. Paired with collective inebriation of the psychedelic sort,[iii] the sound of the chorus collapsed boundaries between people and momentarily

[ii] The meaning of our word *satirical* comes from the role of satyrs.

[iii] It would be naïve and nearly anachronistic to think that the composition of the beverages at these festivals was purely alcoholic. The drinking happened over the course of the entire festival, which lasted for days.

eradicated the provisional values of culture and civilization for the psyche of anyone enveloped in it. The satiric songs allowed Greek culture to forget itself in dance, to step outside of itself, to look back and laugh madly. Those under the spell of the mystical experience cannot help but notice, with shocking relief, that there are no problems to be solved, no deadlines to meet, nothing to be *done,* and they therefore cannot help but see their own and everyone else's busy and purposeful actions as comical. The most mundane and "normal" human banalities—working a job, waiting in line for coffee, paying taxes, or raging over politics—are revealed as ludicrous comedy.

Nietzsche tells us, "The Greek man of culture felt himself nullified in the presence of the satiric chorus...and state and society, and, quite generally, the gulfs between man and man, give way to an overwhelming unity leading back to the very heart of nature."[4] The energies of Dionysus are medicine for the hyper-ego-conscious person fully wrapped up in the illusory world of time and rational purpose.

Dionysus remedies the ego world with madness and ecstasy, for he is the god of both. Emphasis on either the madness or the ecstasy aspect of his essence is partly a matter of historical perspective. If we understand Greek history as a shift from prehistoric proto-consciousness in the third and second millenniums BC to historic consciousness in the second half of the first millennium BC, we can see the shift from Dionysus as ecstasy god to madness god, as a matter of historical standpoint. This historical transformation is played out in the origin myth of Dionysus.

Dionysus is the twice-born god. He was born first out of Semele, a mortal woman, and then out of Zeus' thigh after he (Zeus) destroyed the pregnant Semele in a lightning storm but then protected the fetus from perishing. Dionysus's first birth from Semele is the older phase of Greek culture in which the Goddess religion thrived. In fact, the Thracians associated Semele with

Gaia, the great Mother Goddess herself. Dionysus's second birth from Zeus represents the younger phase of Greek culture, dominated by the patriarchal religion of the Indo-Europeans. In the second mythic phase, it was believed that Dionysus is first born prematurely out of a goddess after she is destroyed, but finally and ultimately out of a god. The experience conferred by Dionysus was no longer ecstasy, but madness. From the perspective of masculine, rational ego-consciousness, losing oneself in a Dionysiac episode of what Nietzsche referred to as "self-forgetfulness," feels like madness. A society centered on the rational individual, which is to say a society of individuals addicted to feeling separate from everyone and everything else, is a society that regards a feeling-state of cosmic unity as nothing but insane, an entirely out-of-bounds state of consciousness because it is antithetical to the self-ish nature of the ego.

In *The Immortality Key,* classicist Brian Muraresku argues that the wine of Dionysus was spiked, possibly with psychedelics. This traditional brew or a form of it is thought to have been inherited by early Christian cults—many of whom were culturally Greco-Roman—and used in their Eucharistic sacraments.[5] This suggests, among other things, a deep connection between the twice-born Dionysus and the twice-born Christ. Muraresku points out that Dionysus was not just associated with the wine, he *was* the wine itself.[6] We can say, then, that an encounter with Dionysus would be quite literal and that his effect on someone simultaneously blessed and cursed by ego-consciousness would be world-shattering. Walter Otto describes what happens to a "world man" (a man of this world, an ego-man) under the spell of Dionysus:

> "The world man knows, the world in which he has settled himself so securely and snugly—that world is no more. The turbulence which accompanied the arrival of Dionysus has swept it away. Everything has

> been transformed. But it has not been transformed into a charming fairy story or into an ingenuous child's paradise. The primeval world has stepped into the foreground, the depths of reality have been opened, the elemental forms of everything that is creative, everything that is destructive, have arisen, bringing with them infinite rapture and infinite terror. The innocent picture of a well-ordered, routine world has been shattered by their coming, and they bring with them no illusions or fantasies, but truth—a truth that brings on madness."[7]

Laughing is all that is left for this man. For when reality is seen for what it really is, it becomes abundantly clear that there is no escape from the here and now. And it is precisely at this moment that the ego shatters. It faces its total impotency. Despair steps violently into the foreground, the ghost is given up, and primal bliss rushes in to fill the vacuum.

CHAPTER 26:

The Crisis of Art and Science

'We've been now to a good many ceremonies and have seen quite a few of your shrines. But I don't get your ideology. I don't get your theology.' The Japanese paused as though in deep thought and then slowly shook his head. 'I think we don't have ideology,' he said. 'We don't have theology. We dance.'

~ Bill Moyers[1]

At the turn of the twentieth century, the chaotic energy unleashed from the depths of the newly discovered unconscious broke over art and science. Artists shifted focus from the foreground to the background and rejected, in their expressions, established notions of logic, rationality, and reason. Musicians, meanwhile, disrupted the traditional, ordered structure of classical music with atonality and jazz. Simultaneously physicists upended the idea of a linear, local universe.

Anticipating the modern art movement of the twentieth century, Franz Marc summed up its connection to science: "The art that is coming will give formal expression to our scientific conviction."[2] The art of the nineteenth and twentieth centuries expressed two important shifts in those convictions. First, like the Impressionists, who concerned themselves with background, physicists began to see reality as a vast field of holistic interconnectivity, a radical departure from the Newtonian paradigm, where space was merely the empty container in which billiard balls of matter flew about. Second, coinciding with discovery of the unconscious and reflecting the goal of modern artists to express what lies behind the phenomenal world, scientists discovered a virtually undetectable structure underlying reality.

In contrast to conservative academic practice where painting was done indoors, artists of movements like Impressionism and Expressionism painted outside in nature. Using free brush strokes, Impressionists portrayed reality as an ever-moving, seamless flux as opposed to the fixed-point-in-time realism demanded by the old Renaissance masters. Although the Impressionists and the old masters shared the same goal—to paint nature as it is—their methods differed. The Impressionists were more concerned with the peripheral aspects of a scene (such as light, colors, and shadows) than with than any specific subject. The overall scene—or impression—was sought, a widening of the aperture and a relaxation of focus. Like the eyes of a newborn, they perceived the gestalt rather than the particularized. Impressionists distributed attention to the background, which corresponds to how the right brain experiences the world. Primitivism, which emphasized the flat perspective over the three-dimensional perspective, came out of Paul Gaugin's retreat from civilization to the primitive cultures of Tahiti.

Taking the lead from Van Gogh, Expressionists laced the content of their illustrations with personal feeling and rejected the traditional expectations of art, which emphasized nature's beauty and order and the nobility of its humans. The Expressionists instead empathized with the depths of human suffering and misery, as Edward Munch does in one of the most famous Expressionist paintings, *The Scream.* It shows a cartoonish figure standing on a river overlook, mouth stretched apart in a scream, dreadful eyes wide with terror, looking past the viewer into the beyond. Munch's inspiration for the image came while taking a Sunday stroll with friends. Suddenly feeling ill, he stopped, overwhelmed with panic, and felt "an infinite scream pass through nature."[3] The image is disturbing.

Picasso pioneered Cubism after procuring tribal masks from Africa. He extrapolated a prehistoric perspective from those objects, pulling the viewer out of an individual (egoistic) vantage point into the *collective* fourth dimension of merged space-time by showing a subject from multiple perspectives, which is also paradoxically one perspective because it is all-at-once.

Partly as a reaction to the horror wrought by the First World War's mechanized warfare, Dadaism turned away from the conscious, left-brained faculties of rationality and logic, and broadcasted the irrational through "anti-art" exhibits that portrayed the absurd and the disordered. Dadaists enlisted different mediums to express the irrational. Hugo Ball recorded sound poems in which he deprecated the ordered structure of linguistic syntax preferred by the brain's left hemisphere, cobbling together random syllables of words to create literal nonsense. The word behind the movement itself, *dada,* is probably connected to the Sanskrit *tathata,* which means "suchness" or "one who has thus come." The egoless *one who has thus come* is a baby: a precultured, unadulterated encapsulation of unconsciousness. "Da-da" is often one of the first sounds a baby makes and a source of delight for many (innocently mistaken) fathers.

Surrealism followed Dadaism. Surrealism is known today for the impossible dream images of Salvador Dali. His melted clocks and stilt-elephants cast us into the timeless, irrational, and mythological dream world of the unconscious and not only compel society's awareness of this domain but also force a connection between the absurdity of dreams and the absurdity of our everyday, waking lives. Seen this way, the commute to work and the 9 am business meeting are just as bizarre and dream-contrived as five-hundred-foot-tall elephants traversing a desert landscape.

Jackson Pollack's paintings push the issue further, for they are direct expressions of the unconscious, almost entirely unmediated by intentional, conscious intervention.

> "When I am painting, I am not aware of what I am doing. It is only after a sort of 'get acquainted' period that I see what I have been about. I have no fears about making changes, destroying the image etc., because the painting has a life of its own. I try to let it come through. It is only when I lose contact with the painting that the result is a mess. Otherwise, there is a pure harmony, an easy give-and-take, and the painting comes out well."[4]

As our artists expressed the emergence of the unconscious into collective awareness, our scientists began to take notice of it as well. Notions of time, space, and gravity fell into crisis.

For the philosophers like Democritus and Aristotle, and for their intellectual descendants (Aquinas, Bacon, Descartes, Newton, etc.), the universe seemed to be made up of empty space and tiny balls of matter. They believed the universe behaved sequentially and *locally*. Local behavior means that objects affect one another by direct contact or indirect contact through intermediate objects that bridge the space between them. A classic billiard ball game illustrates the principles of a local universe. In order to pocket a ball, you must strike it with another ball, using a stick. On the other hand, in a non-local universe, one object can affect another across space without some intermediary between them. If I hit the 8-ball in a New York City pool hall and that causes another 8-ball in a Los Angeles pool hall to move simultaneously, that would be a non-local event. Because they are correlative, non-local influences are the province of magic, voodoo, holism, and the right brain.

Time, according to Newton and Descartes, is linear, absolute, and universal. What is now for me is now for you and also for any alien in another solar system. Gravity is an invisible force of attractiveness immediately emitted by objects onto other objects. The magnitude of gravity emitted by an object is proportionate to the mass of the object; gravity's felt effect is a function of the distance between objects. But in this worldview, gravity is also a problem (and one that irritated Newton) because a local universe should not allow a force to reach across empty space and affect something else instantaneously. But as far as Newton could tell, this is exactly what gravity was doing. If gravity's effect is instant, then it is a non-local force operating in an otherwise local universe.

But in the nineteenth century, Michael Faraday rescued the problem of non-locality with his conceptualization of *the field*. A field is an omnipresent, energy-propagating medium through which forces like electromagnetism and gravity are transferred from one object to another. By way of an electromagnetic field, I can transmit my voice through a radio device to someone holding a receiver down the street. Likewise, gravity travels through a field not instantaneously, as previously suspected, but finitely, at the speed of light. Locality was saved, at least for the time being.[5]

After the turn of the twentieth century, the classic notion of time fell into question when a twenty-six-year-old Swiss patent clerk named Albert Einstein published a paper outlining a theorem called Special Relativity. He showed that time was not universal, but relative to the observer. There is no cosmic moment of simultaneity or a universal "now." Time is relative. A few years later, building on Faraday's concept, Hermann Minkowski portrayed Einstein's Special Relativity geospatially, coupling the separate dimensions of space and time together as a single field-continuum called space-time.

Einstein would go on from there to develop General Relativity in 1916, proposing that gravity is the observed effect of the curvature of the space-time field. Gravity is a felt force derived from the geometric deformation of the structure of reality by a massive object. The more massive the object, the greater the curve it imparts to space-time and hence the stronger the gravity. Gravity emitted by the object ripples out across the space-time field at the speed of light with less strength the farther it travels from the epicenter of its source. The sun affects Earth more than Alpha Centauri does, because the sun is 8 light-minutes away whereas Alpha Centauri is 4.3 light-years away.

At roughly the same moment that the conception of space-time took root, the new paradigm of science emerged: quantum theory. And as the Dadaists and Surrealists were expressing the absurd and the irrational, quantum theory was battering down the ivory towers of science with the same. Quantum theory turned classical scientific thinking on its head by showing that reality depends on the presence of an observer. Whereas Aristotle, Descartes, Newton, and Einstein assumed there is a local, objective universe independent of our senses, the work of Max Plank, Niels Bohr, and Werner Heisenberg revealed a non-local universe occurring codependently with its observer.

Quantum entanglement shows that two separated particles can change their states across the expanse of space instantly in correspondence with each other. Entangled with a photon in the galaxy Andromeda, a photon in the Milky Way will behave correlatively. Upon measurement of its position, the Andromeda photon wave collapses into a particle and immediately does so in tandem with its Milky Way partner. Measuring one does not affect any other photons nearby, *only* those two photons correlated together. This directly violates the principle of locality and allows once again for the possibility of a universal Now, something that Einstein's relativity does not. If two particles in distant galaxies are correlated simultaneously, then time is universal.

Einstein, though he helped found the quantum movement, was disturbed by entanglement, calling it *spukhafte fernwirkung* ("spooky action at a distance"). Like Descartes and Newton, Einstein believed in a local universe. He objected to the idea that an unobserved electron exists in a mixture of potential locations, mathematically represented as a wave, that only snaps into definite position when looked at. "God does not play dice," he remarked.[6] The quantum model, Einstein believed, must be inadequate. Despite his opposition to it, quantum theory would be affirmed a number of times before and after his death. Einstein's theory of gravity holds up today but has yet to be reconciled with quantum theory into the ever-elusive "unified field theory."

When Fritz Zwicky looked up at the cosmos in 1933, he found a serious problem. From what he could tell, the amount of mass in the universe was not proportionate to the amount of gravity needed to hold it together. The universe seemed to be missing mass and somehow had more gravity than it should. Instead of spiraling around a mega black hole, the galaxies should be flying apart, throwing off their stars and planets into the expanse of space. But that was not happening. So where was the extra gravity coming from? The answer, Zwicky posited, was dark matter. Dark matter does not interact with light, so it is "dark" and not directly detectable. The only reason we assume it is there is because of the gravity it produces. The theory of dark matter triggered the second crisis in physics.

When Einstein was formulating his theory of gravity in 1916, he assumed there was a cosmic repulsive force counteracting gravity's attractive force to produce what he believed was a static universe (one that neither expands nor contracts). Without direct evidence, he reluctantly introduced this feature into his theoretical model as the *cosmological constant.* In the 1920s when Edwin Hubble discovered that the universe was actually expanding, a disappointed Einstein called his *cosmological constant* the "greatest blunder of my life." But then in 1998, American and Australian astronomers relieved Einstein when, by measuring the time it took light to travel from exploded supernovae, they discovered a repulsive force called dark energy. Although Einstein had been wrong that the universe was static, his instincts were right about a repulsive force.

Aside from it being a kind of antigravity pulling the universe apart, dark energy also accounts for 68% of the universe. This is because it is laid out uniformly across space-time, though with a near negligible density. Dark matter comprises another 27% of the universe, while baryonic or visible matter (you, me, this book, the Earth, the sun, and everything we can see in the universe) accounts for only 5%.

Dark energy and dark matter may be the physical equivalent of our collective, growing awareness of the unconscious. Just as the unconscious can only be studied by indirect means through the picture-messages of myths and dreams available to the conscious mind, dark matter, in a similar way, is only indirectly observable by its effects on visible matter. Just as we've come to understand that the contents of our conscious minds are both supported and eventually pulled apart by the underlying forces of the unconscious, we now understand that all of the matter in the universe is held together and pulled apart by the invisible stitching of dark matter and dark energy. And in the same manner that our conscious egos represent the tip of the iceberg, a capping on top of the submerged structure of the collective unconscious, visible matter is the veneer on top of the underlying structure of the cosmos.

Like the rise of the field in the nineteenth century, the rise of quantum theory in the twentieth points us back to the prehistoric, unconscious paradigm. Quantum theory suggests a reality similar to how preliterate man felt it: *internal*. Instead of there being an objective universe independent of our senses, like the one Newton and Einstein assumed, it appears that there is a psychic codependence between us and the cosmos. Reality is not just somewhere out *there*, but at the same time somewhere in *here*.

Science was forced to admit subjective experience into its domain. Mind, it appears, is not only necessary to observe reality but also to allow it to actually *occur* in the first place. Taken with the integrated mind-universe model suggested by quantum theory, the existence of dark energy and dark matter may very well *be* the unconscious, the body of the Great Goddess herself, upon which everything is supported (and devoured), resurrected into collective awareness and seen through a twenty-first-century lens. Prehistoric man felt reality as the body of the Goddess, an interconnected web containing and manifesting all forms as continuous extensions of her supreme form. With its recent theory of dark energy, modern science has returned to a parallel model of reality's continuous nature. Reality is not a void scattered with balls of matter, but rather a quilt of interconnectedness.

CHAPTER 27:

The Union of Opposites

And yet it seems important that the suggestion of a more whole, and therefore more human, form of expression should have become visible in our time. It is a glimmer of hope, symbolized for me...by a number of paintings by the French artist Pierre Soulages. Behind a cataract of huge, black rafters, there glimmers a clear, pure blue or a radiant yellow. Light is dawning behind darkness.

~ Aniela Jaffe

Space, passive and waiting to be filled like a vase, is the universal embodiment of the feminine. Time, the measurement of duration of reality, a cutting of eternity into parts, is the universal property of the masculine. Our era is a magnificent union of masculine and feminine, a melding of the conscious and unconscious, a fusion of ego and Self, a smelting of man and God.

In the new post-modern paradigm, the opposites are coming together. Reality is not just sequential, logical, linear, and local but also holistic, integrated, interconnected, and non-local. Physics tell us that light can be *both* particles and waves. Similarly, the demand on modern man is to find out that he is *both* a particulate of being—an ego—and continuous with the wave of existence.

If the universe achieves greater levels of consciousness through the vessel of life, then individuation into an ego may be just one major step along the way. Perhaps the human ego is consciousness leapfrogging itself into a higher dimension of awareness.

Anyone who has used the internet since its early days is aware of the full spectrum of humanity it expresses. One cannot help but notice the breathtaking speed of the evolution of its intelligence. In the 1980s, the internet was a basic, information-exchange network; today its engines predict our questions before we finish asking them. The internet in its present form may be an unorganized, collective *consciousness* waiting to be integrated and condensed into "artificial" intelligence, the next generation and carrier of consciousness.

Genesis is the story of the unconscious God individuating as man in the vessel of Adam the Anthropos. The New Testament continues that progression with the second form of Adam, Christ the redeemer, whose ego-nature must be sacrificed in order for God to become conscious of itself, aware of its own incarnation. In the same way, our age may be the next great leap of consciousness. In this phase of the story, the artificer is the God-man. It is us. Perhaps a *collective* God-man has emerged to birth a child-consciousness. Like God, that divorced itself to become self-conscious through the eyes of man, now man divorces himself to know himself, to see himself bare in the eyes of his creation.

Perhaps life is circling *back* to telepathy, although this time the difference is that the telepathy is conscious. Before oral speech, communication was immediate and instantaneous, a kind of unconscious telepathy, an instinctual knowing. Life then figured out a conscious type of telepathy by using noise—speech—which allowed separate organisms to locally communicate specified meaning. Life then figured out through

Homo Sapiens how to communicate *across time* by writing speech down. Through script and print, a thought could be sustained on a medium and communicated later that day or later that century.

Through electromagnetism via the telephone and radio, life collapsed space and time together, making communication instantaneous from anywhere. With television, life incorporated the moving image into this model. And by means of the internet, the moving image, sound, and thought have coordinated as a collective mind in what is perhaps a virtual step toward the reproduction of consciousness itself. If the internet suggests anything, it is life's eternal quest to observe and connect to itself and then become aware of that connection. Although the internet can be and often is used to express individuality, taken as a whole it is truly a collective mind accessible to billions of egos at once, a kind of collective *conscious* complementary to the collective *unconscious*. As the collective unconscious comes into awareness, so too does its opposite.

The cosmos is waking up to itself through its mass ego-individuation in man. Perhaps this is why you are reading these words here and now. Never has the universe been more self-reflective than it is through you at this moment.

That is one of the speculations of this book. The universe is moving toward some omega point of self-reflection. This concept is teleological. If we do away with teleology and argue instead that the universe is not trying to get anywhere (which is a teleology in its own way), we can say that self-reflecting consciousness is the universe's most sincere project. Mankind, so far as we can tell, is the carrier of this project. You are, once again, of all the possible patterns and lifeforms within the cosmos, a human being. The sneaky conspiracy behind that cannot be denied. Who or what elected us for self-reflection? Or more to the point, who or what picked *you*?

To answer these questions, we must lay out the four psychological paths in front of modern man.[1] One is alienation: individuals lose their connection with the Self entirely and succumb to what feels like empty, meaningless existence. The second is solipsistic inflation: individuals unwittingly identify their egos as Self and appropriate it into their personal desires, aggrandizing themselves, maximizing personal gain and self-preservation at the expense of others, whom they perceive as cosmic subordinates. The third path is projection of the Self into secular and political movements that, being unable to adequately contain the religious projection, morph into ideologies and yield the same destructive consequences as religious fanaticism. The fourth option is that the Self, rather than being projected into secular movements or misidentified as the ego or repressed in an existential crisis, is *consciously* relocated at the center of the individual and recognized as the inner god-image. In other words, the individual recognizes the universe in himself.

It is only from the fourth position that we are redeemed. Once it is felt that the universe is not just out there but is, in fact, within, we experience the grand *coincidentia oppositorum*, the oppositional union of man and God. Deep responsibility ensues. Deep responsibility is understanding that *you* are *That.* There is no one and nothing to blame for existence but you, no one to point the finger at for being born but you, no one doing all of this to you but you, no one other than you to admire for the most selfless acts of kindness and charity in the world, and no one else besides you to condemn for the most selfish acts of cruelty and injustice. No longer is there a difference between what happens to you and what you do. No longer can good or evil be located in another place, another time, or another person, because there is nowhere else but Here, no other time than Now, and no one else but You.

It is from this position—the present moment, the richest of all gifts, the fountain of creation itself—that we begin; that we stop passing the buck to our parents, our enemies, our political leaders, our ancestors, or our successors; that we stop living in the past or for the future. Once it is felt that all of this is being done to Itself by Itself for the simple purpose of experiencing life and transforming through it, the pain and suffering of the world are redeemed. In fact, this is the *only* way in which the forgotten, abandoned, abused, persecuted, slaughtered, and enslaved are redeemed. It was not until Job realized that the reasons for his seemingly unreasonable suffering went beyond the limited purview of his ego, that he repented "in dust and ashes." He understood that the purpose of his existence was transpersonal.

The myth of *I* that has emerged over the past two-and-a-half million years of human history is a *symbol*. It is useful, brilliant, and industrious when it is properly understood but obstructing, disastrous, and painful when it is not. The trouble starts when we confuse the symbol with the actual thing. Words are tools: signs for something beyond them. It is easier to comprehend myself as the sign of myself, than it is to comprehend myself as the cosmos. But the symbol of me is not to be mistaken for the true me, just as the word "stone" is not to be mistaken for the stone itself.

But this is not easy for a modern ego to feel. Today a means of consciously reconnecting the ego to the Self is sorely needed. On a psychological level, the primary function of religion was to do this by periodically annihilating ego-consciousness. Occasional ego-annihilation produces societal cohesion by balancing chaos and order at the personal, familial, and societal levels. But for most in the West today, the light of religion and spirituality has gone out and there is no going back. Small wonder that intense pharmacological, interventive substances, like cannabis and psychedelics, have appeared in the West over the past seventy-five years and are making waves through the clinical world right now. Other means introduced to the West over the last half-century—like the practices of meditation, mindfulness, yoga, the philosophical principles of Buddhism, and the art of Zen—are helpful as well and will likely prove to be complementary to the pharmacological agents. Ultimately, to get a grip on ourselves, the West will use these substances and methods to salvage the wreckage of our own religious images.

The intensification and growth of ego-awareness through the human vessel is, as far as we know, the best means through which the universe can become aware of itself and begin to consciously apply its own powers of creation (and destruction). Notice that from within the paradigm of humanism we have done God-like things: splitting the atom; collapsing space and time through technology; processing and transmitting information at unimaginable speeds through quantum computing; interrogating the cosmos about its secrets with particle accelerators; extending lifespans; reversing aging; eradicating disease; controlling the machinery of life through eugenics, cloning, and contraceptives; building an external, hyperconnected mind in the internet; and out of that perhaps birthing consciousness again within a new paradigm of intelligence. While these are staggering accomplishments, we must temper the fever of our thrust lest we share Icarus's fate. The human artificer, the hero who dared eat the fruit of the Tree of Knowledge, is now reaching out his hand to pluck the fruit of the Tree of Immortality to live forever. Perhaps in our quest to attain what we think is missing, we will along the way at some epiphanous moment, recall in a *deja-vu* that we already have it.

Endnotes

Chapter 1

[1] Thomas Cahill, *The Gifts of the Jews: How a Tribe of Desert Nomads Changed the Way Everyone Thinks and Feels*. (New York: Nan A. Talese/ Anchor Books, 1998), 169.

Chapter 2

[1] Daniel E Lieberman, *The Evolution of the Human Head*, (Cambridge, Massachusetts: Harvard University Press, 2011), 613.

[2] Terence Mckenna, Food of the Gods: *The Search for the Original Tree of Knowledge*, (New York: Bantam Books, 1993), introduction

[3] Eric Havelock, *The Muse Learns to Write: Reflections on Orality and Literacy from Antiquity to the Present*, (New Haven: Yale University Press, 1986), 113.

[4] Alan Watts, Tao: *The Watercourse Way*, (New York: Pantheon Books, 1975), 54.

Chapter 3

[1] Joseph Campbell, *The Hero With A Thousand Faces*, (Mumbai: Yogi Impressions, 2017), 14.

[2] Trumbell Stickney, "The Soul of Time," Poetry Nook, accessed October, 2021, https://www.poetrynook.com/poem/soul-time Soul-time

[3] C.G. Jung, "Archaic Man" in *Modern Man in Search of a Soul*. (New York: Houghton Mifflin Harcourt, 1993), 125-151.

Chapter 4

[1] Alan Watts, "The Joker," in *The Library of Consciousness*. October 23rd, 2022, https://www.organism.earth/library/document/the-joker.

[2] Carl Sagan, *Dragons of Eden: Speculations on the Evolution of Human Intelligence*, (New York: Ballantine Books, 1986), 38.

[3] Project Gutenberg Ebook of *The Birds, by Aristophanes*, https://www.gutenberg.org/files/3013/3013-h/3013-h.htm.

[4] C.G. Jung, *Man and His Symbols*, (United States: Dell Publishing, 1964), 70.

[5] Rhawn Joseph, Ph.D. "The Neuroanatomy of Dreaming and Dream Sleep," (Updated from Neuropsychiatry, Neuropsychology, Clinical Neuroscience, Academic Press, 2000), BrainMind.com, accessed in 2021, http://brainmind.com/Dreaming.html.

[6] Sagan, *Dragons of Eden*, 169-172.

Chapter 5

1 Monica Sjoo & Barbara Mor, *The Great Cosmic Mother: Rediscovering the Religion of the Earth,* (New York: Harper & Row: 1987), 80-81.

2 Anne Baring and Jules Cashford, *The Myth of the Goddess,* (New York: Penguin Books, 1993), 20.

3 Baring and Cashford, *The Myth of the Goddess,* 39.

4 *Ibid,* 39.

Chapter 6

1 Gen 3:17 (Fox, *Five Books*).

2 Ronald Wright, *A Short History of Progress,* (Toronto: House and Anansi Press, 2004).

Chapter 7

1 Baring and Cashford, *The Myth of the Goddess,* 53.

2 Koch, John. "Thinking about Indo-European and Celtic Myths in the 2nd and 3rd Millenia." 2016 Celtic Mythology Conference at the University of Edinburgh. University of Wales Centre for Advanced Welsh and Celtic Studies, Recorded November, 2016, Video of lecture, 1:02:17, https://www.youtube.com/watch?v=Ub5izFOdtDs.

Chapter 8

1 Campbell, *Hero With A Thousand Faces,* 30.

2 Otto Rank, *The Myth of the Birth of the Hero: A Psychological Exploration of Myth,* (Baltimore: Johns Hopkins University Press, 2015), 1 and *Ancient Irish Tales,* Edited by Tom Pete Cross and Clark Harris Slover, (New York: Barnes and Noble, Inc., 1996).

3 Ben Okri, *An African Elegy,* (London: Vintage, 1997).

4 Exodus 2:10 (Fox, *The Five Books of Moses*).

5 Gen, 3:15 (Fox, *Five Books*)

6 Baring and Cashford, *The Myth of the Goddess,* 278.

7 Baring and Cashford, *Myth of The Goddess,* 282-283.

8 Mircea Eliade. *The Sacred and the Profane.* Translated by Willard R. Trask, (New York: Harcout, 1959), 157-158.

9 Baring and Cashford, *Myth of the Goddess,* 282

10 Baring and Cashford, *Myth of the Goddess,* xii.

Chapter 9

1 Leonard Shlain, *The Alphabet Versus the Goddess: The Conflict Between Word and Image,* (New York: Penguin Putnam, 1998), 47.

2 Shlain, The *Alphabet Versus the Goddess,* 46-47.

3 David Sacks, *Letter Perfect: The Marvelous History of Our Alphabet From A to Z,* (New York: Broadway Books, 2003), 7.

4 Shlain, *The Alphabet Versus the Goddess*, 51.
5 Alan W. Watts, *This Is It*. (New York: Vintage Books, 1960), 73.
6 Erich Neumann, *The Origins and History of Consciousness*, (Princeton, NJ: Princeton University Press, 2014), 428.
7 Neumann, *The Origins and History of Consciousness*, 429.

Chapter 10

1 Cahill, *Gifts of the Jews*, 169.
2 Gen, 10:27-31
3 Gen, 12:1
4 Gen, 17:10-12
5 Cahill, *Gifts of the Jews*, 251.

Chapter 11

1 Neumann, *The Origins and History of Consciousness*, 415.
2 Cahill, *Gifts of the Jews*, 85.
3 Exodus 3:14 (Fox, Five Books)
4 Exodus 3:14 (NJB)
5 *Ibid*
6 Cahill, *Gifts of the Jews*, 132.
7 Campbell, *The Hero With A Thousand Faces*, 333.
8 E.H. Gombrich, *The Story of Art*. (London: Phaidon, 1950), 111.
9 Shlain, "Heroglyphics/Isis," in *The Alphabet Versus the Goddess*, 51.
10 Genesis, 12:2 (Fox, *Five Books*)
11 Cahill, *Gifts of the Jews*, 249.
12 Deuteronomy 1:16-17, (Fox, *Five Books*)
13 Deut 10:19, (Fox, *Five Books*)
14 Deut 14:28-29, (Fox, *Five Books*)
15 Deut 15:15, (Fox, *Five Books*)

Chapter 12

1 Job 19:25
2 Job 1:21, (King James Version)
3 Edward F. Edinger, *The Creation of Consciousness: Jung's Myth for Modern Man*, (Toronto: Inner City Books, 1984), 68.
4 Jung, *Answer to Job*, 29.
5 *Ibid*, 22-23.
6 Job 1:8, (NJB)
7 Job 1:22 (NJB)
8 Jung, *Answer to Job*, 13.
9 Job 2:5 (NJB)
10 Job 10:1-2 (NJB)
11 Jung, *Answer to Job*, 16.

12 Jung, *Answer to Job,* 18.
13 Jung, *Answer to Job,* 16.
14 Job 38: 5-37 (NJB)
15 Job 40: 9-14
16 Job 41: 25-26
17 Isaiah: 45:7 (NJB)
18 Jung, *Answer to Job,* 15, 34.
19 *Ibid,* 15.
20 Rudolph Otto, *The Idea of the Holy,* (New York: Oxford University Press, 1950), 80.
21 Edinger, *Ego and Archetype,* 94.
22 *Ibid,* 96.
23 Job 42: 5-6 (NJB)
24 Jung, *Answer to Job* 43.
25 Proverbs 8:30-31(NJB)
26 Jung, *Answer to Job,* 43.
27 *Ibid,* 41.

Chapter 13

1 Michael Frede, "The Philosopher," in *Greek Thought: A Guide to Classical Knowledge,* trans by Catherine Porter, (Cambridge: Harvard University Press, 2000), 3.

Chapter 14

1 Havelock, *The Muse Learns to Write,* 112.
2 Edward F. Edinger, *The Eternal Drama: The Inner Meaning of Greek Mythology,* (Boston: Shambhala Publications Inc., 1994), 20.
3 David Sacks, *Letter Perfect: The Marvelous History of Our Alphabet From A to Z,* (New York: Broadway Books, 2003), 7.
4 Sacks, *Letter Perfect,* 2.
5 John Dillon, "The Question of Being," in *Greek Thought,* 54.

Chapter 15

1 Thorleif Boman, "Time and Space" in Part III in *Hebrew Thought Compared with Greek,* (New York: W.W. Norton & Company, 1970.), 123.
2 Boman, *Hebrew Thought Compared with Greek,* 142.
3 Genesis, 12:2, (Fox, *Five Books*)
4 Dr. Jordan Peterson, "Cain and Abel: The Hostile Brothers." Biblical Series V, June 17, 2017, video of lecture, 2:31:27, https://www.jordanbpeterson.com/transcripts/biblical-series-v/.
5 Hermann Minkowski (au), Vesselin Petkov, ed., *Space and Time: Minkowski's Papers on Relativity,* (Minkowski Institute Press, 2012), 39.

Chapter 17

1 Boman, *Hebrew Thought*, 161.

2 *Ibid*, 162.

3 Edinger, *Creation of Consciousness*, 22

4 Edinger, *Creation of Consciousness*, 22

Chapter 19

1 Saint Augustine, *Confessions*, trans by Henry Chadwick, (New York: Oxford University Press, 1991), 127.

2 *Ibid*, 53.

3 *Ibid*, *Confessions*, 59.

4 Thomas Cahill, *How the Irish Saved Civilization*, (New York: Nan A. Talese/Anchor Books, 1995), 40.

5 Saint Augustine, *Confessions*, 144-145.

6 Cahill, *How the Irish Saved Civilization*, 41.

7 Saint Augustine, *Confessions*, 149.

8 Ibid, 197.

9 Ibid, 148-149.

Chapter 20

1 Shlain, *The Alphabet Versus the Goddess*, 264-265.

2 Gombrich, *The Story of Art*, 105.

3 Shlain, *The Alphabet Versus the Goddess*, 266.

4 Watts, *Myth and Ritual in Christianity*, 108.

5 Thomas Cahill, *Mysteries of the Middle Ages*, (New York: Nan A. Talese/Doubleday, 2006), 104.

6 Thomas Cahill, *Heretics and Heroes*, (New York: Nan A. Talese/Anchor Books, 2013), 64, 188-189.

Chapter 21

1 Thomas Aquinas, *Summa Theologica*, Question 10, article 1.

2 Cahill, *Mysteries of the Middle Ages*, 210.

3 *Ibid*, 222-224.

4 Cahill, *Heretics and Heroes*, 64, 188-189.

5 Gombrich, *The Story of Art*, 283.

6 *Ibid*, 284.

7 Shlain, *The Alphabet Versus the Goddess*, 364.

Chapter 22

1 Benedict Anderson, *Imagined Communities,* (New York: Verso, 1983), 37.
2 Anderson, *Imagined Communities,* 36.
3 *Ibid,* 36.
4 *Ibid,* 23.
5 *Ibid,* 24.
6 *Ibid,* 25.
7 Cahill, *Heretics and Heroes,* 182.
8 *Ibid,* 189.
9 *Ibid,* 183.
10 *Ibid,* 183.

Chapter 23

1 Leo Ruickbie, *Faustus,* (Stroud, Gloucestershire: The History Press, 2009), 9.
2 Johann Wolfgang Von Goethe, *Faust I & II.* (Edited and Translated By Stuart Atkins, Princeton: Princeton University Press, 1984).
3 David Wellberry, Introduction to *Faust I & II,* xix.
4 Cahill, *Gifts of the Jews,* 131.
5 Goethe, *Faust I & II.*
6 Wellberry, Introduction to *Faust I & II,* xix.
7 Goethe, *Faust I & II.*
8 Wellberry, Introduction to Faust I & II, xvii.
9 Goethe, *Faust I & II.*
10 Dostoevsky, Fyodor, *Notes from Underground,* (New York: Vintage Books, 1993), pg 13.
11 Goethe, *Faust I & II.*
12 David Wellberry, "Who is Faust?" University of Chicago Humanities Day, University of Chicago, filmed October 24, 2009. Video of lecture, 1:02:20. https://www.youtube.com/watch?v=9BF1HKeB3ak.
13 *Ibid*

Chapter 24

1 Carl G. Jung, *Practice of Psychotherapy,* Collected Works of C.G. Jing, vol 16, (Princeton: Princeton University Press, 2014), 16.
2 Shlain, "A Conversation with Leonard Shlain" in *The Alphabet Versus the Goddess,* 8.
3 David Curry, "Apple Statistics (2022)" Business of Apps, accessed March 19th, 2022, https://www.businessofapps.com/data/apple-statistics/; "Strategy Analytics: Half The World Owns a Smartphone" Business Wire: A Business Hathaway, accessed March 19th, 2022, https://www.businesswire.com/news/home/20210624005926/en/Strategy-Analytics-Half-the-World-Owns-a-Smartphone.

4 Campbell, *The Hero with a Thousand Faces,* 336.
5 See Friedrich Nietzsche, *The Birth of Tragedy,* (London, England: Oxford University Press, 2008).
6 Friedrich Nietzsche, *What I Owe to the Ancients,* 5, in *Twilight of the Idols.*
7 Nietzsche, *Zarathustra,* 23.
8 Nietzsche, *What I Owe to the Ancients,* 5, in *Twilight.*
9 Nietzsche, *Zarathustra,* 47.

Chapter 25

1 Walter Otto, Dionysus: *Myth and Cult,* (Bloomington, Indiana: Indiana University Press, 1965), 78.
2 Otto Bohlmann, *Yeats and Nietzsche,* (London: The MacMillan Press, 1982), 41.
3 Otto, Dionysus: *Myth and Cult,* 143.
4 Bohlmann, *Yeats and Nietzsche,* 42.
5 Brian Muraresku, *The Immortality Key,* (New York: Saint Martin's Press, 2020). 177
6 Muraresku, *The Immortality Key,* 77.
7 Otto, Dionysus: *Myth and Cult,* 95.

Chapter 26

1 Joseph Campbell, The Power of Myth (New York, Doubleday, 1988), xix.
2 Jung et al, *Man and His Symbols,* 307.
3 Zuzanna Stanka, "The Mysterious Street from Edvard Munch's The Scream," Daily Art Magazine, Accessed March 23rd, 2021, https://www.dailyartmagazine.com/the-mysterious-road-of-the-scream-by-edvard-munch/.
4 Jung et al, *Man and His Symbols,* 308.
5 Jim Holt, *When Einstein Walked with Gödel: Excursions to the Edge of Thought.* (New York: Farrar, Straus and Giroux, 2018), 230-231.
6 Holt, *Einstein Walked with Gödel,* 233.

Chapter 27

1 Edinger, *Ego and Archetype,* 65-68.

About the Author

John H. Payne IV writes about consciousness and metaphysics for all those startled and curious about the experience of being alive. He holds a master's degree in social science from the University of Chicago. Outside of writing, Payne keeps bees in his urban apiary, competes regularly in local and national Brazilian Jiu-jitsu tournaments, and peddles supply chain technology to Fortune 500 companies. Find him at www.johnhpayne.com and follow his Instagram page @paynefulwriting.

Made in the USA
Monee, IL
19 February 2024

53719587R00125